DEDICATION

I dedicate this book to two very special men: C. S. Lewis, you know; Don Giovanni Calabria was a Catholic Priest. The two men never met, nor did they share a common language, yet they found a way to correspond in Latin for several years shortly after WWII ended. Those letters greatly encouraged me in the writing of this book and gave me the standard that I applied to every page of *The Eighth Day: Being Christian in a Sixth-Day World.*

> I have tried to do the only thing I think myself able to do: that is, to leave completely aside the subtler questions about which the Roman Church and Protestants disagree among themselves—things which are to be treated of by Bishops and learned men—and in my own books to expound, rather, those things which still, by God's grace, after so many sins and errors, are shared by us.

> - C. S. Lewis, Letter 2, Magdalen College Oxford, 6th September 1947 to "Reverend Father," Verona, Italy

C. S. Lewis and Don Giovanni Calabria, *The Latin Letters of C. S. Lewis*, Translated and edited by Martin Moynihan (South Bend, Indiana: St. Augustine's Press, 1998) 33.

Contents

THE EIGHTH DAY

In the very beginning, Christians were known simply as The Way. In Antioch, we were first called Christians (Acts 11:26). But early on in church history and tradition, they began speaking of an eighth day, a day which symbolizes the Kingdom of God as it resides eternally above and beyond the limitations of even the seven days of the Creation itself. Eight is a highly symbolic number in all of Holy Scripture for Christians—but most importantly, of these four things:

1. By Judaic Law, on the eighth day after his birth, Jesus was circumcised, thus joining him to the Prophets and to the Law, to Abraham and to Moses, and to God's Covenant with Israel.

2. On the eighth day of His Passion Week, Jesus opened the doors of Heaven for us when He physically rose from the dead and redeemed mankind—on the eighth day of the Passion Week, on Sunday, which is the first day of God's new and everlasting Creation.

3. The numbering of our days will reach its conclusion with the setting of the sun on the Sixth Day; on the Seventh Day, He will revive us; on the Eighth Day, He will raise us up just as He was resurrected.

> Come, and let us return unto the Lord: for he hath torn, and he will heal us; he hath smitten, and he will bind us up.

> After two days will he revive us: in the third day he will raise us up, and we shall live in his sight (Hos 6:1-2).

4. The Passion Week also parallels the Genesis account of the days of creation as follows:

On the Sixth Day of the Creation, God created mankind (male and female created He them), and mankind rebelled against the authority of its Creator. In the New Testament account of the sixth day of the Passion Week (our Friday), Jesus paid the penalty for mankind's sin as He took our judgment upon Himself.

On the Seventh Day of the Creation, God rested. On the seventh day of the Passion Week, during the commanded Jewish Sabbath day of rest (our Saturday), Christ's body rested in its tomb—thus, Jesus fulfilled all the commandments of God on our behalf.

On the Eighth Day of His Passion Week (our Sunday), Christ's bodily resurrection becomes Christianity's Eighth Day of the Creation, which is the First Day of the New Creation. Heaven's gate is unlocked, and we are invited inside for the Marriage Feast of the Lamb, not as guests, but as the Bride of the Feast—Christ the Bridegroom and the Church, His Bride. And from this Holy Union, the Universal Church is born, that church which lives above and beyond even the seven days of the Creation. "And he that sat upon the throne said, Behold, I make all things new" (Rev 21:5 KJV).

> And so it is written, The first man Adam was made a living soul; the last Adam was made a quickening spirit (I Cor 15:45).

> And as we have borne the image of the earthy, we shall also bear the image of the heavenly (I Cor 15.49).

While this book is about a number of different things, it is all about authority: God's absolute authority and undeniable will for His Creation—and Judeo-Christianity's rather large part to play in that will today.

THE COMMON BODY OF CHRIST

In the latter half of the first millennium, a man named Cynewulf summarized centuries of Christian belief in a beautiful Anglo-Saxon poem entitled, *Dream of the Rood* (Cross):

Then the young hero prepared himself,

That was Almighty God,

Strong and firm of mood,

he mounted the lofty cross courageously,

in the sight of many,

when he willed to redeem mankind.[1]

We are the Church Universal. We are Judeo-Christianity, the Bride of the Marriage Feast. We are the oldest of the trees of the Creation, the Tree of Life, which is filled with the fruits of God's Holy Spirit, our many branches reaching out for Heaven, the light of Heaven itself falling upon us daily, the moon of Heaven warming us even through our coldest and darkest nights. Our roots travel back in time to before the creation of time itself. Our history is recorded within the primordial waters of the Biblical Book of Genesis and is fulfilled within the vision of St. John's Revelation, wherein created time flows back into Uncreated Timelessness. We are the intrinsic, living, organic, visible witness to time, of Eternity. We are the Common Body of Christ.

Ecumenism means let's understand one another—let's talk.

Syncretism means let's become one another—let's merge.

This book is *Ecumenical* in that it is structured on the sure knowledge that Christianity adheres to a common faith and a common Scripture upon which we can build a common dialog— and we can start that conversation with Gal 2:20-21.

> I am crucified with Christ: nevertheless I live; yet not I, but Christ liveth in me: and the life which I now live in the flesh I live by the faith of the Son of God, who loved me, and gave himself for me.

> I do not frustrate the grace of God: for if righteousness come by the law, then Christ is dead in vain (Gal 2:20-21 KJV).

Many popular modern translations read "faith in the Son of God," but the *King James Version,* "I live by the faith of the Son of God," expands that meaning to resting not upon our own pitiful and wavering faith in Christ but resting in Christ's own absolute faith and trust in His Father. If Christ indeed lives His life and will within us now, and if we indeed are dead to the world and set apart from the world in Him, then living "by the faith of the Son of God" is to live out Christ's own faith in the Father. His faith elevates us far beyond what any poor faith of ours could ever achieve. This is the power that is manifested in the lives of the great saints and martyrs. And this same power is available to all Christians everywhere and under all circumstances.

The *American Standard Version* of the above verse reads:

> I have been crucified with Christ; and it is no longer I that live, but Christ living in me: and that life which I now live in the flesh I live in faith, the faith which is in the Son of God, who loved me, and gave himself up for me. I do not make void the grace of God: for if righteousness is through the law, then Christ died for nought (Gal 2:20-21 ASV).

Complete this thought with the same verse from the *Revised Standard Version-Second Catholic Edition (the Ignatius Bible),* which states it this way:

> I have been crucified with Christ; it is no longer I who live, but Christ who lives in me; and the life I now live in the flesh I live by faith in the Son of God, who loved me and gave himself for me. I do not nullify the grace of God; for if justification were through the law, then Christ died to no purpose (Gal 2:20-21 RSV-2CE).

Once again, this time from *The Orthodox Study Bible (OSB) St. Athanasius Academy of Orthodox Theology*, whose chosen New Testament is the *New King James Version*:

> I have been crucified with Christ; it is no longer I who live, but Christ lives in me; and the *life* which I now live in the flesh I live by faith in the Son of God, who loved me and gave Himself for me. I do not set aside the grace of God; for if righteousness *comes* through the law, then Christ died in vain (Gal 2:20-21 NKJV).

And from the popular Protestant *New International Version*:

> I have been crucified with Christ and I no longer live, but Christ lives in me. The life I now live in the body, I live by faith in the Son of God, who loved me and gave himself for me. I do not set aside the grace of God, for if righteousness could be gained through the law, Christ died for nothing (Gal 2:20-21 NIV).

Same, same, same, same and same: Scripture plants the staff of the Universal Church in all its denominations and divisions right here and within the meaning of these verses. As Christians are united forever to Christ and Christ is united forever to His Bride, so also, through Him, are we united forever to one another. This book is a celebration of that Holy Communion.

When looking for a translation of the Bible that would become the backbone of this book, I ran into multiple copyright, permissions, and uses problems until I finally came to BibleGateway.com, looking for a conservative translation that was still in the Public Domain. What I rediscovered there was my first true love, the *King James Version*. I have included the credits for the above five Biblical versions as part of the Introduction because of their importance to the Introduction itself.

"The King James Version present on the Bible Gateway matches the 1987 printing. The KJV is public domain in the United States."

https://www.biblegateway.com/versions/King-James-Version-KJV-Bible/

This version is used throughout this book unless noted otherwise. ('Conservative' as used here means a close *literal accuracy* translation—one which has not been compromised by today's modern ideology or politics.)

The American Standard Version (ASV), which is also in the public domain, will be used only as a complimentary version added to the text when more clarification is needed; and it will always be noted as such.

The American Standard Version (ASV), Copyright © 1901, is in the Public Domain. Accessed 19 May 2014, on Biblegateway.com

http://www.biblegateway.com/passage/?search=Gal%202:20&version=ASV

For a third, I have chosen another conservative version. The *Revised Standard Version-Second Catholic Edition (RSV-2CE or The Ignatius Edition)* which incorporates and maintains the integrity of the 1952 *Revised Standard Version of the Bible (RSV)*—not coincidentally "an authorized revision of the *American Standard Version*, published in 1901, which was a revision of the *King James Version*, published in 1611." (Hopefully, you see how they all tie in together.) This version is a highly readable Bible, but it will appear only once, in the Introduction, because of copyright limitations and is noted as such. This is not the version found on Biblegateway.com, but a later, slightly more conservative version of the Catholic Edition, which *is* found there.

Revised Standard Version Bible, Ignatius Edition, Copyright © 2006, Division of Christian Education of the National Council of the Churches of Christ in the United States of America.

Fourth, and only once in the Introduction is the *Orthodox Study Bible's (OSB) New Testament* from Thomas Nelson's *New King James Version* quoted:

Scripture taken from the New King James Version®. Copyright © 1982 by Thomas Nelson. Used by permission. All rights reserved.

Only once, again, and to confirm that Gal 2:20-21 is the same in all of the mainstream Christian Churches, is the popular NIV quoted:

Whether you are Protestant, Reformed, Catholic, or Orthodox, this is *our* Holy Bible, and it is the root of our common knowledge of God, our salvation, one another, and especially of His will for all of us. Read it. Understand it. Believe it. Live it. And you will fall in love with the God Who wrote it.

And it came to pass, as he sat at meat with them, he took bread, and blessed it, and brake, and gave to them.

And their eyes were opened, and they knew him; and he vanished out of their sight.

And they said one to another, Did not our heart burn within us, while he talked with us by the way, and while he opened to us the Scriptures?

And they rose up the same hour, and returned to Jerusalem, and found the eleven gathered together, and them that were with them,

Saying, The Lord is risen indeed, and hath appeared to Simon.

And they told what things were done in the way, and how he was known of them in breaking of bread.

And as they thus spake, Jesus himself stood in the midst of them, and saith unto them, Peace be unto you (Luke 24:30-36 KJV).

SECTION I

BEGINNINGS

Lord, thou hast been our dwelling place in all generations.

Before the mountains were brought forth, or ever thou hadst formed the earth and the world, even from everlasting to everlasting, thou art God.

Thou turnest man to destruction; and sayest, Return, ye children of men. For a thousand years in thy sight are but as yesterday when it is past and as a watch in the night (Ps 90:1-4).

1

GENESIS, CREATION AND QUINTESSENCE

THE FIFTH ELEMENT

"It is written," Jesus replied three times to the Adversary.

"It is written," Judeo-Christianity proclaims.

"It is written," in the Old Testament of the Hebrew Bible.

"It is written," in Christianity's New Testament.

"It is written," into the very heart of the Creation itself—*God's absolute authority over all that He has created.*

In the beginning God created the heaven and the earth.

And the earth was without form, and void; and darkness was upon the face of the deep. And the Spirit of God moved upon the face of the waters.

And God said, Let there be light: and there was light (Gen 1:1-3).

What was the first commandment that God gave to His Creation? Don't eat fruit from that tree over there? Not even close. It was the Law before the Law of Day One, the basic law which anchors the other laws of physics: "Let there be light" (Gen 1:3). It would have taken the Word of God speaking the energy equivalent of just those four words to bring forth the intense energy which exploded into created light, matter, space and time. Just those four words spoken into the primordial waters of chaos brought enough energy to continuously support, maintain, contain and infuse all that they created. The law which physics depends upon so heavily is that delimiting speed of created light which not only forms but is the boundary of, the Creation.

Who would not love to brood over the primordial waters with God and watch as He speaks creation into them? And who would not long to dive into God's great ocean of truth and discover the endless, the limitless, the eternal treasures contained in it? Judeo-Christianity has always taught that God has given us two essential gifts so that we can come to know Him: the perfection of the Creation itself and the perfection of His Divine revelations. We come to the fullness of the knowledge of God and of our own existence, the Universal Church declares, by both faith and reason.

1. Quintessence: The fifth element in physics, but the first and most essential element of the Creation, which is both essence and act.

2. Quintessential Act: Earth, air, fire, water, and the pure quintessential act which brought them into being—and by which their existence is justified and sustained.

3. Quintessential Force: The force that is causing and governing the acceleration of the universe's continuing expansion.

4. Quintessential Physical Law: That One Law which writes all the other laws of physics:

> In the beginning was the Word, and the Word was with God, and the Word was God.

> The same was in the beginning with God.

> All things were made by him;

> and without him was not any thing made that was made (John 1:1-3).

This chapter goes back to the very beginning of The Creation and then simply lets God reveal Himself through what He has created.

> Day 1: Light: the energy of creation (created light, matter, space and time)

> Day 4: Sun, Moon, Planets, Stars

> Day 2: The waters and the skies of the earth

> Day 5: Water Creatures and Fowls of the air

> Day 3: Dry Land and Plants

Day 6: Land Animals and Mankind

In the first three days, God created the regions: the heavens, the waters and the land are divided from one another into three separate stages. This is followed by the creation of the occupants of those regions—listed in the same order that their domains were generated, but later. Now then, that's reasonable and so is this:

> The heavens declare the glory of God; and the firmament sheweth his handywork.
>
> Day unto day uttereth speech, and night unto night sheweth knowledge.
>
> There is no speech nor language, where their voice is not heard.
>
> Their line is gone out through all the earth, and their words to the end of the world. In them hath he set a tabernacle for the sun,
>
> Which is as a bridegroom coming out of his chamber, and rejoiceth as a strong man to run a race (Ps 19:1-5).

God delights in revealing Himself to us through His works, and it is exciting to celebrate a rapidly evolving science as it grows up to a university level on the physical plane. Far from proving that there is no God, even secular science is now coming to the awareness of a beginning of all things. Indications are that Someone or Something must have written the supreme law, that law which governs, controls and is the foundation and framework for all the other laws of the physical world—that which many call "the theory of everything." And it appears that we are going back to the belief that there must have been some quintessential act that not only produced a very beginning but through which our continuing existence is made possible and sustainable—and if a quintessential act, then a quintessential Actor.

Bit by bit, God is proving a rational universe to a rational world and even the most skeptical among us are beginning to discover that there is an Ultimate Reality from which all reality derives its being. From DNA to digestive systems, mankind explores itself as an integral part of the whole of the physical creation. We *are* little bits of stardust, but stardust into which God breathed living souls. "And the Lord God formed man of the dust of the ground, and breathed into his nostrils the breath of life; and man became a living soul" (Gen 2:7).

But we also understand scientific skepticism because even Thomas the Apostle was a skeptic:

> The other disciples therefore said unto him, We have seen the Lord. But he said unto them, Except I shall see in his hands the print of the nails, and put my finger into the print of the nails, and thrust my hand into his side, I will not believe (John 20:25).

So the Lord God gave mankind a telescope and a microscope:

> For the invisible things of him from the creation of the world are clearly seen, being understood by the things that are made, even his eternal power and Godhead; so that they are without excuse:

> Because that, when they knew God, they glorified him not as God, neither were thankful; but became vain in their imaginations, and their foolish heart was darkened (Rom 1:20-21).

With the Word's spoken energy and the creation of light and the speed of light, and using matter, space and time as constants—but wait, are these really constants? It is just here that many of our misunderstandings begin. Can it really be the familiar and measurable earth time, clock and calendar time that we are thinking of when we read Genesis? Or is that space time? When you throw in variables against time such as mass, gravitational forces and velocities, time seems to bend, stretch, collapse, speed up or slow down, and sometimes even to tear apart, disappear, and go off our screens altogether as it takes light, space and matter right along with it. So, how would it be possible to measure the time of Creation's Genesis with our clocks and calendars, seasons and days, when our universe was still receiving all its bits and pieces and our twenty-four-hour solar day was still a long way off? Was this God's light and darkness, evening and morning—time as seen from the perspective of eternity where the end can be constantly seen from the beginning?

If we are to successfully explore the Creation, we need to think through once more what God has already revealed to us and go back to a simple definition of time which encompasses all of its complicated known and unknown variables:

Time is the visible, measurable motion of the
ongoing act of creation.

Time means that you must have a Primary Actor if you have a primary act that not only sets all things in motion (since time is motion) but holds all things together in motion—a Creator who is the only absolute constant of His creation. Motion cannot come from nothingness. The motion of time must come from a timeless Somethingness. And we know through revelation that time will not always be with us and that it will ultimately end—but only when its purpose is fulfilled.

Creation is not only beautiful, reasonable and understandable, but with a gigantic paintbrush, God has painted His own astounding self-portrait in it. So then, is it all just superstition in the face of today's science? Or is it manifested to each one of us, each night and day—and in every way possible, has God made Himself obvious?

The Lord by wisdom hath founded the earth; by understanding hath he established the heavens.

By his knowledge the depths are broken up, and the clouds drop down the dew (Prov 3:19-20).

Here are a few more questions to round out this chapter: Did God simply set the ball of creation rolling and then become indifferent to it? Are we living in a closed system, unique within ourselves and thereby prone to a disorder that will eventually destroy us, a sort of entropy that makes us fall victim to all sorts of random effects and influences from time? Will time itself become spent energy? And if so, does that mean that the original creative source of energy spoken into existence, in the beginning, can be, or will be, spent to exhaustion?

We can answer all of these questions with a single answer: The problem that we have here with applying the second law of thermodynamics to the physical laws of creation is that we don't live in a closed system. The motion of creation (time) is completely shot through and through with huge holes and there is Eternal Energy leaking into time just everywhere—and that fact challenges all the equations to grow into something greater than the most brilliant mind using the most advanced technologies could ever hope to calculate.

One more important fact to consider here: The very act of creating establishes not only the ownership but the absolute authority of the Creator over what He has created.

And that leads us into the next chapter.

2

ARE WE EVOLVING?

When God's Authority is Questioned

Rule #1. Accept God's absolute authority and trust Him in all things.

Rule #2. Understand that there are no other rules.

If we can recognize the primary laws in the running of the universe and in the order of nature, then why can we not recognize the primary laws for the order of mankind? These laws, these pesky rules, were given not to take our freedom from us but to create a structure within which our freedom could flourish and grow. These rules that were designed to keep us safe and free from error were written into our hearts at the beginning of our creation. This is called the Natural Law, the law that tells us that there is right and there is wrong. There is no truth unless it is the absolute and unchangeable truth that comes only from the absolute and unchangeable authority of God. To demonstrate this, we will have to go all the way back to what actually took place in the Garden of Eden and the part it played in the design of the Creation itself.

The unique creation of Adam was a most perfect act. He was made perfect in body and mind, spirit and soul, thought, intelligence and reason so that he could communicate with his Maker. Through Adam, we who are alive today inherit that same invitation to walk every step of every day in God's Garden with Him. We are the natural explorers and scientists that we are because we were made not only to care for the Creation but to understand it by unraveling its wonderful mysteries—God creating for man to discover, name, organize, care for, and delight in what He has made.

We are destined not only to be fully at home within the physical creation but also to comprehend our own unique place in it—even now—even while we must still reside in this day, the Sixth Day of the Creation. The joy of discovery was mandated for us at our beginning, through the race of Adam, and this order was never rescinded. And as we are still living within the motion of the ongoing act of God creating, we are still living in the Sixth Day of the Creation.

For now, we will cause time's multidirectional movement to go in only in one direction, and that is forward, the direction that mankind must live within it on planet earth. If you draw a very short line in the middle of a large sheet of white paper, the line would have a beginning, a middle and an end, but the paper itself would be the platform that supports and surrounds the line. The short line represents our time. The paper would be statically present to all points on the line all at once, while the motion of time must move along the line created for it. The paper, if extended infinitely out in every direction, represents eternity--- timelessness.

Timeless Eternity is constantly present to the beginning, to the middle and to the end of created time; therefore, God is with us now, still creating His Sixth Day. God is also present at our beginning while simultaneously waiting for us at our end. He knows our past, our present and our future because being the Eternal I AM, He is always present to all of Creation. From this constant presence of God comes all existence.

So, what does this mean to us personally? It means that we didn't miss the big show of creation after all. Even today, even now, we are living witnesses to a physical creation that is still in its Sixth Day phase—and so are we.

When Adam (a term meaning both male and female) entered the world of time, decay and death, this was not the ascent of Adam but the descent of Adam and all which would be born from our first parents. There was only one question that God had asked of the couple and it is the same question that He asks of us today: Will you accept My authority and trust Me in all things, even when you don't understand? Our first parents replied "No" when they chose their own desires over the authority of God's one commandment.

This is our first indication of why we should protect the sacred truth of Scripture exactly as it has been handed down to us— protect it without ever compromising, challenging or changing it so that it will fit more politically and correctly into whatever current world thinking is popular? Sin works first of all by changing the truth, if only slightly, and this is how it worked in the Garden of Eden. Someone added just five simple, seemingly harmless words to the original command that God gave to Adam. Read the original, and then read Eve's revision of the original:

> And the Lord God commanded the man, saying, Of every tree of the garden thou mayest freely eat:

> But of the tree of the knowledge of good and evil, thou shalt not eat of it: for in the day that thou eatest thereof thou shalt surely die (Gen 2:16-17).

That seems simple and straight forward enough, but when the Serpent asked Eve, "Yea, hath God said, Ye shall not eat of every tree of the garden?" (Gen 3:1), he got more than he ever hoped for when Eve replied:

> We may eat of the fruit of the trees of the garden:

> But of the fruit of the tree which is in the midst of the garden, God hath said, Ye shall not eat of it, *neither shall ye touch it*, lest ye die" (Gen 3:2-3). (Italics mine.)

Five seemingly innocent and well-intentioned words had been added to the original commandment: *neither shall ye touch it*. The

Serpent had but to get Eve to touch the tree and the fruit upon it and live. Then Eve had but to eat the fruit and live to entice her husband.

Are we not smarter than a serpent?

Did you notice how I changed the Serpent's identity by changing just one word in the above question? I changed *the* to *a?* *A* serpent is just any old snake (*a* being an indefinite article), but *the* Serpent can only mean our Adversary in this story (*the* being a definite article, the identifying article in this case). We don't have to be smarter than the Serpent; all we must do is to wholly accept and trust in the wisdom of God, nothing added, nothing taken away, nothing superimposed, and nothing, once again, compromised or changed. Be careful with Scripture because changing very little can change a whole lot.

> And the serpent said unto the woman, Ye shall not surely die:

> For God doth know that in the day ye eat thereof, then your eyes shall be opened, and ye shall be as gods, knowing good and evil" (Gen 3:4-5).

He had just subtlety suggested that God wanted to keep them subordinate children in ignorant bliss. But how could it be wrong if it made one wise like God? In fact, how could it be wrong if we can become god-like ourselves?

And when the woman saw that the tree was good for food, and that it was pleasant to the eyes, and a tree to be desired to make one wise, she took of the fruit thereof, and did eat, and gave also unto her husband with her; and he did eat" (Gen 3:6).

Adam and Eve had no anthropologist to describe the human condition to them. They had no history for a reference point, had been given only the one commandment and had never experienced disobedience before. The advisor that Eve chose was a creature already in fallen rebellion, but there was no Bible to tell her so. She was created after the law had been given, and when Adam passed it down to her, he must have strengthened it with a warning (or she simply assumed the warning) to not "touch the fruit," which was not in the original commandment. Then strangely, Adam is silent in Eve's temptation. Adam's original sin may have been his silence in the garden during Eve's temptation—not the sin of commission, but the sin of omission as in the general confessional, "in what I have done and in what I have failed to do." Was Adam even there and close enough to stop her? And if not, then why, once she fell into disobedience, did he follow her? Was it his love for her or was it the desire to be "like God" that convinced him to eat the fruit—or was it something else altogether?

The Apostle Paul says that the woman was deceived by the Serpent, but Adam was not, leading some to suggest that it was his love for Eve that seduced him to enter into and to share her fate as Christ entered into our condition and shared ours, even to the point of separation from the Father: "My God, my God, why hast thou forsaken me?" (Matt 27:46). Did Adam already have a revelation of the love and the mercy of God as well as of the judgment of God, as some teach? If so, he had a strange way of showing it when he immediately and without hesitation laid the blame for the trespass not only upon his wife, but upon God Himself: "And the man said, The woman whom thou gavest to be with me, she gave me of the tree, and I did eat" (Gen 3:12).

In a type and anti-type understanding of Scripture, the Son of God, for love of His Bride, the Christ without sin, followed us into the wilderness of our disobedience and took our sins and our judgment upon Himself—*but never did He partake of our sin as Adam did of Eve's sin.*

The death sentence given to Adam and Eve was the first indication of the inestimable mercy of God. He knew that to allow the couple to live forever in a world which was struggling eternally with temptation, disobedience, sin, violence and death would make life intolerable for them and for all their generations to come. For their sakes and the sake of all of their children, the Tree of Life would become the Cross of the Sacrifice of Jesus, the Christ of God, and the antidote for the poison fruit of sin. This is My Body. This is My Blood. The Christ of God offers us the salvific gift of

Himself as we partake of Christ's sacrifice in Holy Communion even today.

> He that hath an ear, let him hear what the Spirit saith unto the churches; To him that overcometh will I give to eat of the tree of life, which is in the midst of the paradise of God (Rev 2:7).

As the knowledge of good and evil woke up to its first dawn, Adam and Eve gathered their things together and walked reluctantly out of the Garden of Eden in their new coats of skin as immortality took on the problems of mortality. The couple had just made their first truly important discovery and Adam quickly penciled it into his catalog of names. God Himself would erase the record later with the entry into time of the Savior of Mankind: "And I will put enmity between thee and the woman, and between thy seed and her seed; it shall bruise thy head, and thou shalt bruise his heel" (Gen 3:15).

Common Names: Satan, The Serpent, The Devil, Lucifer

Kingdom: Spirit

Division: Angel

Class: Fallen

Order: Adversarial

Family: Demonic

Genus: Darkness

Species: Enemy

Identifying trait: Lies and Deceptions

Day two of the knowledge of good and evil: The firstborn of Adam became the first murderer; and the second born of Adam became the first martyr.

Adam and Eve did not enter into the world of time until they left the Garden of Eden, and when they left, they were without genetic defects or hereditary imbalances. Even their new coats of skin were created to self-regenerate and to self-heal so that they really could have lived for centuries upon centuries in a way that we can only dream of in the world of passing time, death and decay. Adam ruled and was contemporary with his sons and grandsons to the seventh generation. Our first parents were not suddenly given the brain of an ape or the skills of a caveman with their new coats of skin. And by the time of Noah, even those children of Adam who had sinned by marrying into the world of mankind had incredible descendants.

3

THE FLOOD

Type and Antitype in the Bible

In this chapter, we begin demonstrating type and antitype as they appear throughout the whole of the Bible. The Old Covenant (Testament) is the type, the prefigurement or foreshadowing of the New Covenant (Testament), which is the antitype or the fulfillment and realization of that type. There are so many promises, covenants, types and antitypes between the Old and the New Testament that it will take a few more chapters to explain and address this important subject. Here are the two most important ones that apply to the Christ of God.

> And so it is written, The first man Adam was made a living soul; the last Adam was made a quickening spirit (I Cor 15:45).

> And the Lord God caused a deep sleep to fall upon Adam, and he slept: and he took one of his ribs, and closed up the flesh instead thereof;

> And the rib, which the Lord God had taken from man, made he a woman, and brought her unto the man.
>
> And Adam said, This is now bone of my bones, and flesh of my flesh: she shall be called Woman, because she was taken out of Man (Gen 2:21-23).

The type is self-explanatory: Eve was born from the wounded side of Adam. The antitype is the fulfillment of that type: The Church is born from the water and the blood which flowed from the wounded side of Christ—reborn as the Bride of Christ. This is important enough to our understanding of Scripture that we should repeat it: 1. Adam's side was wounded so that Eve could be born; and 2. Christ's side was wounded so that His Bride, the Church, could be born.

This is the most perfect example of type and antitype in the Bible, but it is overflowing with others. Covenants, types and antitypes are not just teaching parables written down by the prophets of God—they are God Himself illustrating His truths and authority through the lives of and events of real people.

In *To Heal a Fractured World, The Ethics of Responsibility*, Rabbi Jonathan Sacks explains the importance of the Hebrew Bible for all of us:

> The Bible is God's call to human responsibility . . . Freedom, choice, moral agency, accountability, merit, guilt, retributive justice, atonement and forgiveness are

interlocking concepts that were born together, and have their genesis in the Hebrew Bible.[1]

The Bible has given science a written basis for understanding the world before the devastating and all-encompassing flood and the Noachian (Noah's) Covenant that followed it. Those times when we find bits and pieces of a truly advanced civilization from antiquity along with the bones of some more primitive culture that existed long, long ago, we can go back to Genesis and find the stories of these "sons of God" who produced offspring "with the daughters of men" and get a fresh insight into creation history.

> And it came to pass, when men began to multiply on the face of the earth, and daughters were born unto them,
>
> That the sons of God saw the daughters of men that they were fair; and they took them wives of all which they chose.
>
> And the Lord said, My spirit shall not always strive with man, for that he also is flesh: yet his days shall be an hundred and twenty years.
>
> There were giants in the earth in those days; and also after that, when the sons of God came in unto the daughters of men, and they bare children to them, the same became mighty men which were of old, men of renown (Gen 6:1-4).

To equate the generational tribe of Adam to men from Mars or fallen angels from the heavens coming to earth to have sex with a tribe of evolving apes is to become susceptible to all manner of lies and deceptions—it is, in fact, ridiculous and even heretical.

So then, who were these sons of God and where can we find them in Scripture? They were the descendants of Adam: "Noah, the son of Lamech, the son of Methuselah, the son of Enoch, the son of Jared, the son of Mahalaleel, the son of Cainan, the son of Enos, the son of Seth, the son of Adam, the son of God" (Luke 3:37-38 ASV).

If you read it carefully, the account of creation that is found in Chapter 2 of Genesis is not a second account of the Creation, but its first account, a much older history of God creating our first parents, Adam and his wife Eve. "That which is born of the flesh is flesh, and that which is born of the Spirit is spirit" (John 3:6).

These are the generations of the heavens and of the earth when they were created, in the day that the Lord God made the earth and the heavens, And every plant of the field before it was in the earth, and every herb of the field before it grew: for the Lord God had not caused it to rain upon the earth, and there was not a man to till the ground. But there went up a mist from the earth, and watered the whole face of the ground.

And the Lord God formed man of the dust of the ground, and breathed into his nostrils the breath of life; and man became a living soul. And the Lord God planted a garden eastward in Eden; and there he put the man whom he had formed.

And out of the ground made the Lord God to grow every tree that is pleasant to the sight, and good for food; the tree of life also in the midst of the garden, and the tree of knowledge of good and evil (Gen 2:4-9).

Before the plants, before the rains, and before mankind (male and female) were created, God created Adam and Eve. But He did not just speak them into existence—Adam became a living *soul* when the breath of God entered him, and that is what makes us truly different from the rest of the Creation. Adam was formed before the other land creatures and was, therefore, a living eyewitness to their creation.

And out of the ground the Lord God formed every beast of the field, and every fowl of the air; and brought them unto Adam to see what he would call them: and whatsoever Adam called every living creature, that was the name thereof. And Adam gave names to all cattle, and to the fowl of the air, and to every beast of the field; but for Adam there was not found an help meet for him (Gen 2:19-20).

Within the two different accounts of the Creation, Genesis 1 and Genesis 2 (perfect examples of type and antitype), all of these other people who were lost in the flood are explained: the "daughters of men" (the wife of Cain, the feared persecutors of Cain): "I shall be a fugitive and a vagabond in the earth; and it shall come to pass, that every one that findeth me shall slay me" (Gen 4:14).

In Genesis Chapter One, we have documentation of God creating mankind as caretakers of the earth and all that is in it:

> And God said, Let us make man in our image, after our likeness: and let them have dominion over the fish of the sea, and over the fowl of the air, and over the cattle, and over all the earth, and over every creeping thing that creepeth upon the earth.
>
> So God created man in his own image, in the image of God created he him; male and female created he them.
>
> And God blessed them, and God said unto them, Be fruitful, and multiply, and replenish the earth, and subdue it: and have dominion over the fish of the sea, and over the fowl of the air, and over every living thing that moveth upon the earth.
>
> And God said, Behold, I have given you every herb bearing seed, which is upon the face of all the earth, and every tree, in the which is the fruit of a tree yielding seed; to you it shall be for meat (Gen 1:26-29).

This second account of mankind being created in Genesis 1, the mankind which God made, He made in His image, thereby giving to this higher creation authority and dominion over all the rest of earth's creation. He told them to be fruitful and to multiply and to replenish the earth, and He gave them *"every herb bearing seed"* and every tree *"in the which is the fruit of a tree yielding seed" for food.* (Italics mine.) Man was created man (male and female) from the first, neither a pollywog nor an ape. But in the Genesis 1 account of God creating, there is no mention of the forbidden fruit and the forbidden tree, or of the Adversary, or of the fall, or of the curse that was the result of that fall. This Mankind, complete and entire, was created in God's image (with His authority) to care for the earth. The image of God given to these people gifted them with the power to think on their own, to have their own individual personalities, maturities, accountabilities, responsibilities and understandings within themselves and with others—and with God. This is the generation of man whose life span was limited to 120 years and whose existence perished in the flood: "And the Lord said, My spirit shall not always strive with man, for that he also is flesh: yet his days shall be an hundred and twenty years" (Gen 6:3).

This is not to start a debate about creation's order, but to demonstrate something that is essential to understanding many of the principles of the Bible, which are discussed fuller throughout this book: type and antitype. The creation story of the mankind found in Genesis 1 (which became so wicked that it had to be destroyed) finds its antitype in Revelation's doomed City of Babylon. The creation of Adam (male and female) in Genesis 2, who were formed and brought to life with the breath of God, with the Holy Spirit of God, is a foreshadowing of the redeemed of the New Jerusalem of Revelation.

And God saw that the wickedness of man was great in the earth, and that every imagination of the thoughts of his heart was only evil continually.

And it repented the Lord that he had made man on the earth, and it grieved him at his heart.

And the Lord said, I will destroy man whom I have created from the face of the earth; both man, and beast, and the creeping thing, and the fowls of the air; for it repenteth me that I have made them.

Contrast mankind's 120 years with those long-life spans of the Adamic race. In A Dictionary of the Bible, under the heading "Chronology," John Davis presents several ancient accounting systems, one of which counts years by dynasty; i.e., Adam's dynasty would have lasted for 930 years from the moment that Adam descended into the world of time to when it ended at his death.[2] Now, using any of the systems and calendars that you can think of, imagine all the advances that mankind has made in the last 100 years, and then try to imagine what the early Adamic race could have accomplished within the Patriarchs' great and extended lifetimes. Think of the enormous skill, knowledge, wisdom and understanding that had been handed down to them from generation to generation. In all things, physically and intellectually, the Adamic race from Adam to Noah was incredibly advanced, so there is no mystery when we find faint traces and stories of these great civilizations. But the dynasties of mankind, even when interbred with the sons of God, finally became so terrible that they brought Heaven's great foot of judgment crashing down upon the earth.

> In the six hundredth year of Noah's life, in the second month, the seventeenth day of the month, the same day were all the fountains of the great deep broken up, and the windows of heaven were opened (Gen 7:11).

The flood, which wiped out all but eight people from Adam's tribe, was not a little pitter-patter of rain for forty days and nights as is commonly found in children's picture books. This was something immense! Could this be when the tectonic plates jolted dramatically, pouring water through gigantic fissures in some great catastrophic event—violent earthquakes and world-wide tsunamis, the earth rising into mountains, and mountains sinking into the depths of the seas? Were the great and ancient cities lost to the ocean's floor or ground beneath the crust of the earth, or will we eventually be able to find at least some remnant of them beneath the residue of our natural history? Are we just beginning to find these civilizations now in the sands of our deserts and on the ocean's floor? Could this have been the momentous time when the continents began to separate and drift? And what does it tell us about future judgments?

But there is more still: Should we be searching beneath the ocean's floor for something more valuable than oil? Perhaps, fresh rainwater, trapped there ever since the great flood? Once we know Biblical History, the gifts it offers are immense.

> And it shall come to pass, that he who fleeth from the noise of the fear shall fall into the pit; and he that cometh up out of the midst of the pit shall be taken in the snare: for the windows from on high are open, and the foundations of the earth do shake.
>
> The earth is utterly broken down, the earth is clean dissolved, the earth is moved exceedingly (Is 24:18-19).

That would have been a wild ride for the ark, but it was God who summoned those into it who were to be saved; it was God who sealed them in; it was God who unsealed them and called them forth again; it was God's hand that protected this precious and chosen seed for the New Beginning. Most probably, the animals went into hibernation for the duration; the stored food would be needed for the landing, the seeds for sowing, plants for planting until the earth sprouted again. Noah and his family could keep a watch over their precious cargo. The animals that God chose to accompany Noah in the ark would have been those that God had called into the ark, which would be immediately needed by him when the flood waters subsided. There is nothing that says that God could not, did not, or does not still today call forth others, even in faraway places, as our Sixth Day continues traveling along the timeline of the Creation. And we, like Adam, are still living witnesses to God creating it.

Adam said "no" to the authority of God, but Noah said "yes"—and was saved from the flood. Centuries later, this same submission to God's authority would result in the greatest blessing ever known when Eve finds her type within her antitype, in Mary, the Mother of the Christ Child. Where Eve had said "no" to the absolute authority of her Creator and closed the door to the Tree of Life, the New Eve, Mary, says "yes" to God and opened it up again. All through Scripture, we find the continuing theme of those who accept and trust in God's authority and those who refuse it: Jesus and Adam; Mary and Eve; Noah building the Ark which would carry the seed of Adam into its new beginning—and those who refused to enter into it.

And Mary said, Behold the handmaid of the Lord; be it unto me according to thy word (Luke 1:38).

O my Father, if this cup may not pass away from me, except I drink it, thy will be done (Matt 26:42).

And God saw that the wickedness of man was great in the earth, and that every imagination of the thoughts of his heart was only evil continually (Gen 6:5).

But Noah found grace in the eyes of the Lord (Gen 6:8).

4

MELCHIZEDEK

FROM THE OLD ADAM TO THE NEW ADAM

Not many of us will ever read the genealogies found in the Bible and fewer still will make a study of them. And yet, within these lists are hidden exquisite treasures of information—treasures for which Christians are forever indebted to our Jewish fathers. One of Abraham's generational grandfathers was Shem, first appearing in the Bible as one of the three sons of Noah, a direct descendent of Noah and therefore also "perfect in his generations" (in his pure and unmixed lineage from Adam):

These are the generations of Noah: Noah was a just man and perfect in his generations, and Noah walked with God. And Noah begat three sons, Shem, Ham, and Japheth (Gen 6:9-10).

Shem was born before the flood and was only a few generations down from Adam, so it shouldn't be surprising that Shem was 600 years old when he died, 500 years after the flood. The last survivor of the incomparable era of the great Adamic Patriarchs, Shem was still living at the time when a generational grandson of his own was born: Abram, in direct line from Noah, in direct line from Seth, in direct line from Adam, "the son of God." Shem is also listed in Luke's genealogy of Jesus:

Shem, the son of Noah, the son of Lamech, the son of Methuselah, the son of Enoch, the son of Jared, the son of Mahalaleel, the son of Cainan,

the son of Enos, the son of Seth, the son of Adam, the son of God (Luke 3:36-38 ASV).

And the sons of Noah, that went forth of the ark, were Shem, and Ham, and Japheth: and Ham is the father of Canaan. These are the three sons of Noah: and of them was the whole earth overspread (Gen 9:18-19).

It was to Shem that Noah gave his blessing of succession. In some versions of Genesis 10:21, Shem is listed as "the brother of Japheth, the elder," but in a great many Bibles, this is translated as "the elder brother of Japheth." With the passing on of the blessing, Noah also put the houses of his other two sons under Shem's authority and protection. Then, upon his father's death, Shem not only assumed the right of Patriarch in Adam's descent, but he also assumed the role of "Priest of God Most High" for this ever-growing family of Adam. Many believe that Shem was both priest and king of the great city of Salem, not far from where Abram settled after his separation from Lot when Abram dwelt in the land of Canaan. Here is the passing on of the generational blessing of Noah:

> And Noah awoke from his wine, and knew what his younger son had done unto him.
>
> And he said, Cursed be Canaan; a servant of servants shall he be unto his brethren.
>
> And he said, Blessed be the Lord God of Shem; and Canaan shall be his servant.
>
> God shall enlarge Japheth, and he shall dwell in the tents of Shem; and Canaan shall be his servant.
>
> And Noah lived after the flood three hundred and fifty years.
>
> And all the days of Noah were nine hundred and fifty years: and he died (Gen 9:24-29).

If you accept early Jewish and Christian traditions that Melchizedek (translation: the King of Righteousness or the King of Peace [Salem]) was the title of this great patriarch, then you might also consider that Shem passed the Adamic blessing of succession down to Abram when he came forth to meet him. Nowhere else in the Bible is it recorded that Shem passed the lawful succession down to any of his descendants but to Abraham only.

And Melchizedek king of Salem brought forth bread and wine: and he was the priest of the most high God.

And he blessed him, and said, Blessed be Abram of the most high God, possessor of heaven and earth:

And blessed be the most high God, which hath delivered thine enemies into thy hand. And he gave him tithes of all (Gen 14:18-20).

King David, who was descended from the man who would come to be known as Abraham, as well as a descendent of Shem, the son of Noah, the son of Adam, the son of God, saw that Melchizedek was the prefigurement (type) of the One Who would be the true Melchizedek, the eternal and everlasting King of Righteousness (Peace) and Priest of God Most High, the promised Messiah, the King of all kings and the Lord of all lords. Jesus, who was the Christ of God, was Melchizedek's antitype and the fulfillment of this office.

The Lord said unto my Lord, Sit thou at my right hand, until I make thine enemies thy footstool.

The Lord shall send the rod of thy strength out of Zion: rule thou in the midst of thine enemies.

Thy people shall be willing in the day of thy power, in the beauties of holiness from the womb of the morning: thou hast the dew of thy youth.

The Lord hath sworn, and will not repent, Thou art a priest for ever after the order of Melchizedek (Ps 110:1-4).

Initially, Melchizedek simply appears in Scripture with only this title to accompany him. No record of his tribe or ancestry (something unheard of in Jewish histories), no lineage to validate his priesthood (in those days, the priesthood was passed down from father to son), and no record of his death. This led to two assumptions: the first notion is that he might have been an angelic messenger (even though angelic messengers of God cannot be kings, priests, and prophets over Adam), and the second was that Melchizedek might have been the Christ Himself. Scripture as a whole explains that as Jesus was the second and perfect Adam, so was he also the perfection and the fulfillment of the office of Melchizedek—he who was the first official Priest of God Most High ever recorded in Scripture (although Noah did make a thank offering upon leaving the Ark, he was never designated as a priest). Jesus, the King of Righteousness and Peace, is not only our High Priest, but He is also the Sacrifice which has been offered. Jesus is the fulfillment of all the Messianic Prophecies—something that Melchizedek could never do or be. The Christ of God, Jesus, was, therefore, greater than Melchizedek and so was the fulfillment of his office.

Melchizedek was *the* type of Christ in the Old Testament as he came forth from Salem, where he was King, Priest and Prophet. And as he brought forth both bread and wine with which to bless

Abram, he was foreshadowing the sacrifice of the Christ and the initiation of the New Covenant of the Last Supper. Melchizedek's priesthood was not dependent upon a priestly lineage but was both limitless and timeless in its application—in other words. He was a living prophecy, a type of the antitype fulfillment of the Eternal Priesthood of Christ. The genealogy of Shem is listed in Genesis 11 from Shem to Abraham, but his kingdom, his priesthood, and his bread and wine prophecy only foreshadowed the Eternal Kingdom and Priesthood of the Christ of God.

> "Without father, without mother, without descent, having neither beginning of days, nor end of life; but made like unto the Son of God; abideth a priest continually" (Heb 7:3.).

> For this Melchisedec, king of Salem, priest of the most high God, who met Abraham returning from the slaughter of the kings and blessed him;

> To whom also Abraham gave a tenth part of all; first being by interpretation King of righteousness, and after that also King of Salem, which is, King of peace;

> Without father, without mother, without descent, having neither beginning of days, nor end of life, *but made like unto the Son of God*; abideth a priest continually. Now consider how great this man was, unto whom even the patriarch Abraham gave the tenth of the spoils. (Italics mine.)

And verily they that are of the sons of Levi, who receive the office of the priesthood, have a commandment to take tithes of the people according to the law, that is, of their brethren, though they come out of the loins of Abraham:

But he whose descent is not counted from them received tithes of Abraham, and blessed him that had the promises (Heb 7:1-6).

Abram deferred to Melchizedek by paying tithes to him. The Levitical Priesthood would come much later through the carefully recorded lineage of Aaron, brother of Moses. But this offering of tithes from the lesser Patriarch giving to the greater Patriarch, even at this early date, was of major importance because it expanded the promise of salvation beyond just the chosen seed of Abram to include all the seed of Adam represented in the Adamic Patriarch Melchizedek—all races and all tribes and all countries and all tongues—all are in descent from Adam today by reason of the devastation of the flood. Paul, in his letter to the Hebrews, instructs them in this matter "after the similitude of Melchisedek there ariseth another priest":

For it is evident that our Lord sprang out of Juda; of which tribe Moses spake nothing concerning priesthood.

And it is yet far more evident: for that after the similitude of Melchisedec there ariseth another priest,

Who is made, not after the law of a carnal commandment, but after the power of an endless life.

For he testifieth, Thou art a priest for ever after the order of Melchisedec. (Heb 7:14-17).

(The two spellings of the name Melchizedek (Melchisedec) come from the different translations of the two Testaments.)

Jesus Christ is fully God and yet fully the new Adam and the fulfillment of the perfect obedience of the new Adam. He is also both the High Priest and the Sacrifice offered. This One, Who has no beginning and no end, is He Who arises as "another priest" in the similitude of Melchizedek. But Melchizedek was made after the law of a carnal commandment, and therefore, he would die. The One Who would come after him, "another priest," would not be made after the law of a carnal commandment but by the power of an endless life:

1. Melchizedek's *Priesthood* was without lineage, chosen by God, not selected by priestly descent, and continues eternally in Christ the Anointed One.

2. The Kingdom of David would continue forever in Christ the King.

3. The Prophets would find the realization of their prophecies of the Messiah in Christ the Redeemer, who from eternity was and is and will ever be. This is the One in Whom Melchizedek's

blessing to Abraham continues forever and ever, in the Body and the Blood of Christ, in the sacrificial meal of the Last Supper.

Melchizedek is often referred to as the first priest of Christianity because he foreshadowed the Eternal Priesthood of Christ: In Persona Christi, in the person of Christ. The Patriarchal Blessing, which was passed down from Noah to Shem to Abram was sealed with the Bread and the Wine which prefigured the New Covenant of the Last Supper's Body and Blood of Jesus.

Surely there was more to the meeting between generational grandfather and grandson than what was recorded: the two great Patriarchs, the lesser, called out from his people, deferring to the greater who had come out to bless him. Perhaps there would be a long retelling of the story of the Creation, of the fall, of the flood and of a passing down of the promises of a Redeemer by one who had witnessed and experienced the world before the flood, before the deluge. Surely the two Patriarchs camped together for a time. They were relatives, closer now than ever before; surely, they each already knew about the other (Abram would know him to whom he gave tithes).

Abram was called forth from a world of idol worshipers and many gods. He came after the era of the Tower of Babel and after God had scattered the tribes. Here he would learn of the one true God Who had called him out so that he could carry on the witness of his generational grandfathers of old. Surely in a world which had forgotten, this is where Abram learned of the One True and

Living God and of His promises to the race of Adam—Abram, sitting at the table of his grandfather, the Priest of God Most High, the son of Noah, the son of Adam, the son of God. Melchizedek is the bridge that Judeo-Christianity also crosses from the old Adam to the New Adam: Jesus, the Christ of the living God. It was the work, the witness and the lives of the Patriarchs and of the Prophets in the Old Covenant, in the Old Testament, which gave light and understanding to the Apostles of the New Covenant before the New Testament was even written. It is the coming of the Messiah in the New Testament, Who alone can open for us the meaning and understanding of the Old. That is why this obscure little chapter in Genesis is so important and why the genealogies matter.

> Which hope we have as an anchor of the soul, both sure and steadfast, and which entereth into that within the veil;

> Whither the forerunner is for us entered, even Jesus, made an high priest for ever after the order of Melchisedec (Heb 6:19-20).

SECTION II

COVENANTS

Thou carriest them away as with a flood; they are as a sleep: in the morning they are like grass which groweth up. In the morning it flourisheth, and groweth up; in the evening it is cut down, and withereth. For we are consumed by thine anger, and by thy wrath are we troubled (Ps 90:5-7).

5

HEALING THE WORLD

THE CHRISTIAN COVENANT

The term *Abrahamic* faith is used to identify the three great monotheistic faiths that claim Abraham as father. Our purpose in this chapter is to define not only Christianity's relationship to Abraham but Christianity's ties to the prophecies of the Old Testament.

ISLAM claims Abraham (Ibrahim) as father through his first-born son Ishmael (Isma'il), born of Hagar (Hajar), the Egyptian. The true Islamic faith declares the Creation, Adam, Noah, Abraham and Moses, and honors Mary (Maryam), who miraculously gave virgin birth to Jesus, a great prophet. True Islam is the religion that venerates Muhammad as the last of the prophets and adheres to the Holy Qur'an as the foundation of their faith.

JUDAISM claims Abraham through descent from the promised heir Isaac who was born of Sarah, and through Isaac's son Jacob, father of the Israelites—that religion whose covenant with God was sealed by Moses and confirmed by its people at Mount Sinai:

> And he took the book of the covenant, and read in the audience of the people: and they said, All that the Lord hath said will we do, and be obedient.

> And Moses took the blood, and sprinkled it on the people, and said, Behold the blood of the covenant, which the Lord hath made with you concerning all these words (Ex 24:7-8).

CHRISTIANITY claims Abraham as father through our doctrine of Justification by Faith and by our own covenant relationship with God through Jesus, the Son of God, the Redeemer of Mankind, who was promised to the race of Adam in the beginning.

> And he brought him forth abroad, and said, Look now toward heaven, and tell the stars, if thou be able to number them: and he said unto him, So shall thy seed be.

> And he believed in the Lord; and he counted it to him for righteousness (Gen 15:5-6).

The last recorded meeting of Ishmael and Isaac in the Old Testament was when they came together to bury their father.

> And these are the days of the years of Abraham's life which he lived, an hundred threescore and fifteen years. Then Abraham gave up the ghost, and died in a good old age, an

old man, and full of years; and was gathered to his people (Gen 25:7-8).

All the peoples of the earth share a common ancestry from Adam through Noah. Through Adam, all the peoples of the earth inherit God's promise of a Savior, a Messiah, a Redeemer and a Reconciler of mankind with one another and with our Creator: "Male and female created he them; and blessed them, and called their name Adam, in the day when they were created" (Gen 5:2).

Christians can best understand our Covenant relationship with God by first understanding the place that Melchizedek has in our faith. Because Jesus, the Christ of God, is the eternal fulfillment and realization of the office of Melchizedek, Christianity itself, "in persona Christi" (in the person of Christ), does not have a priesthood that is passed down from generational father to son. Paralleling the office of Melchizedek, we can claim our bloodline through Adam and Eve, who, without father or mother, were born of God.

Yet, we are not illegitimate children who were born outside of the successive generations from Abraham, for we claim not only Abraham by faith, but the Messiah through God's promise to our first parents: "And I will put enmity between thee and the woman, and between thy seed and her seed; it shall bruise thy head, and thou shalt bruise his heel" (Gen 3:15).

Can we locate exactly where and when the ancient promises were written into the Christian Covenant? Do you know how our two-sided covenant with God was signed? How it was sealed and to whom it was delivered? And do you know your proper response to it? Do you know how to agree to your part of that bilateral agreement, to this New Covenant, to this New Testament of God? And do you know how you can be certain that Christ's sacrifice for you has been accepted by God?

In order to trace the roots of the Christian Covenant with God, we need to look at the Passion of the Christ again through the Old Testament prophesies before the New Testament was even written.

On the first day of the Passion Week, on Palm Sunday, Jesus entered Jerusalem to a cheering crowd.

> Rejoice greatly, O daughter of Zion; shout, O daughter of Jerusalem: behold, thy King cometh unto thee: he is just, and having salvation; lowly, and riding upon an ass, and upon a colt the foal of an ass (Zech 9: 9).

During the next few days, Jesus curses the fig tree that refused to bear fruit and drives the money changers from the Temple while declaring His Father's house a house of prayer.

> Is this house, which is called by my name, become a den of robbers in your eyes? Behold, even I have seen it, saith the Lord (Jer 7: 11).

The fig tree is found withered, the Sanhedrin are lectured, the Pharisees and scribes are scolded, and Jesus prophesies the destruction of the temple, the end of the age, the Great Tribulation and His future return to judge the nations. The faithful are warned: "Watch therefore: for ye know not what hour your Lord doth come" (Matt 24:42). Jesus is anointed in preparation for His death and burial. Judas cuts a deal with the Chief Priests to betray Jesus and Jesus prophesies his arrest and crucifixion.

Now will I sing to my wellbeloved a song of my beloved touching his vineyard. My wellbeloved hath a vineyard in a very fruitful hill: And he fenced it, and gathered out the stones thereof, and planted it with the choicest vine, and built a tower in the midst of it, and also made a winepress therein: and he looked that it should bring forth grapes, and it brought forth wild grapes (Isa 5: 1-2).

In Judaism, a day is counted from sundown to sundown so that the fifth day of the Passion Week, in Jewish accounting of time, ended at sundown on Thursday.   At sundown on that same Thursday, the sixth day of the Passion Week began at the Passover celebration of the Last Supper, where Jesus once again reveals His impending sacrifice to His disciples. It is here, in this particular place and on this particular night in history, that the Messiah is revealed as that One Perfect and Sacrificial Lamb—the same night in which He was betrayed is the beginning of the same day in which He was crucified (one day not two) the sixth day of the Passion Week, according to Jewish accounting of time: sundown to sundown. Jesus, this day, offered mankind the body and the blood of the New Covenant in fulfillment of the Old Covenant, offered for the forgiveness of sins—the sacrificial offering of His Body and His Blood in atonement for our sins *on the sixth day of the Passion Week*:

> And as they were eating, Jesus took bread, and blessed it, and brake it, and gave it to the disciples, and said, Take, eat; this is my body.
>
> And he took the cup, and gave thanks, and gave it to them, saying, Drink ye all of it;
>
> For this is my blood of the new testament, which is shed for many for the remission of sins (Matt 26:26-28).

And it is here, within the sixth day of the Passion Week that the Christian Covenant with God was prophesied in the Old Testament:

> Then Moses called for all the elders of Israel, and said unto them, Draw out and take you a lamb according to your families, and kill the Passover.
>
> And ye shall take a bunch of hyssop, and dip it in the blood that is in the bason, and strike the lintel and the two side posts with the blood that is in the bason; and none of you shall go out at the door of his house until the morning.
>
> For the Lord will pass through to smite the Egyptians; and when he seeth the blood upon the lintel, and on the two side posts, the Lord will pass over the door, and will not suffer

the destroyer to come in unto your houses to smite you (Ex 12:21-23).

During the night, Jesus wrestles with God the Father in the Garden of Gethsemane in the prayer of His final temptation—wrestles not with the tempter but with the will of the Father. Then, in an all-encompassing surrender of obedience to His Father's will, Jesus fulfills His perfect and final righteousness on our behalf as he gifts us with the second most important prayer, *nevertheless*:

> Father, if thou be willing, remove this cup from me: nevertheless not my will, but thine, be done (Luke 22:42).

In the new Garden, in the Garden of Gethsemane, Jesus becomes the new Adam, the perfect Adam, the surrendered and obedient Adam. On the Altar of the Cross, He becomes the Sacrificial Lamb Who offers His own life and flesh and blood in payment for our sin, providing for us what we could not provide for ourselves—the Passover of the Angel of Death. In the Resurrection, He triumphs not only as Redeemer but as King and High Priest forever "after the order of Melchizedek." Ascending "in the sight of many," He presents to The Father this one perfect and everlasting atonement for the sins of the whole world, His own flesh and His own blood poured out upon the Sacrificial Altar that atones for our sins at Heaven's gate.

Review the Passion Week and the Ascension again and you will see that it is with the Blood of Jesus that the Christian Covenant with God is written upon the Flesh of the Christ of God.

It is with the very public crucifixion, death, burial and sealing of the tomb of the Christ of God that the Christian Covenant with God is witnessed, signed and sealed. It is in the Resurrection that God delivers on what He has covenanted to do from before the beginning of time to save the race of Adam from the death of sin. And as the Resurrection is the sign that the Father has received and accepted this one perfect sacrifice for the atonement of our sins, the wind and the fire of the Holy Spirit being poured forth from Heaven and resting upon the reconciled believers at Pentecost fulfills the promised new beginning for mankind.

Christ's sacrifice has been accepted. We can start over again. We can be born again in the new Adam, the true Adam, the Christ of the Living God. Through faith, we become increasingly infused with the Breath of God, which is the Holy Spirit of God, being conformed to the Image of the Son, not to the image of the natural, but to the Image of the Supranatural, that Image which transcends nature as *time* flows back into *eternity*. We believe, we surrender, and the Lord reckons it to us as righteousness. That's our justification by faith and our baptism is our signature agreeing to that Covenant. But this is more than just a promise or a contract. It is a Personal Covenant Relationship—like an "I Thee wed" marital covenant. And in our Covenant relationship with the Holy Trinity, we become one with one another also, as the one true Bride of Christ: "Is Christ divided?" Well then, neither is His Bride.

But ye are a chosen generation, a royal priesthood, an holy nation, a peculiar people; that ye should shew forth the praises of him who hath called you out of darkness into his marvellous light;

Which in time past were not a people, but are now the people of God: which had not obtained mercy, but now have obtained mercy (1 Pet 2:9-10).

In the Christian Covenant, we have creation and re-creation, sin and redemption, adoption and sanctification and regeneration—as the Holy Spirit of God fills and indwells his Church. Just what more could we ask? Yet, with God, there is always more. It is not enough that we should be washed and born again as babes in a new world. *The meaning of this new life in us is for those born-again babies to grow up!* This path is a long and hard road, but Christ has provided us with the only nourishment that can and will sustain us all the way to its end—the most precious gift of His constant Presence.

And as they were eating, Jesus took bread, and blessed it, and brake it, and gave it to the disciples, and said, Take, eat; this is my body.

And he took the cup, and gave thanks, and gave it to them, saying, Drink ye all of it;

For this is my blood of the new testament, which is shed for many for the remission of sins (Matt 26:26-28).

In the Lord's own words:

> Then Jesus said unto them, Verily, verily, I say unto you, Except ye eat the flesh of the Son of man, and drink his blood, ye have no life in you.

> Whoso eateth my flesh, and drinketh my blood, hath eternal life; and I will raise him up at the last day (John 6:53–54).

> To all of Christianity Paul warns:

> Wherefore whosoever shall eat this bread, and drink this cup of the Lord, unworthily, shall be guilty of the body and blood of the Lord.

> But let a man examine himself, and so let him eat of that bread, and drink of that cup.

> For he that eateth and drinketh unworthily, eateth and drinketh damnation to himself, not discerning the Lord's body (1 Cor 11:27-29).

And to the clergy, Paul strongly advises:

> For I have not shunned to declare unto you all the counsel of God.

> Take heed therefore unto yourselves, and to all the flock, over the which the Holy Ghost hath made you overseers, to feed the church of God, which he hath purchased with his own blood (Acts 20: 27-28).

This does not leave us with an either/or grace or works denominational quandary about Christian salvation, but a definite both: Christ's sacrificial saving grace demands a response on our part—our own sacrificial and unquestioning submission and obedience to Him in reply.

Yet, Christians live in a world of others. We have been sent into the world of others. If the Christian Covenant of salvation is written with the blood of Jesus upon the flesh of Jesus, then what about all these others? What about those good people who have suffered so very much in this world without a chance of ever hearing, let alone accepting or refusing, the Gospel of Christ? And what about the Jews to whom God entrusted so much? *Has God unchosen His Chosen People?*

> Peter seeing him saith to Jesus, Lord, and what shall this man do?

> Jesus saith unto him, If I will that he tarry till I come, what is that to thee? follow thou me (John 21:21-22).

We must begin with the problem of Christian Disunity before we can even begin to tackle the problem of Christian Supersessionism.

6

THE CHURCH DIVIDED

BURYING HATRED

Mohandas K. Gandhi was assassinated in 1948, the same year that Mother Teresa started her ministry in Calcutta and the State of Israel was reborn. Gandhi was intrigued by the beliefs of Christianity—but the reality of the Christians that Gandhi encountered within his lifetime was a society of tradition, a private club in western dress and manner that left no room for cultural differences. There is one story in Gandhi's autobiography which every Christian should read if they haven't already. On his way to see the Kali temple in Calcutta one day, he passed a slaughter of sheep that were being sacrificed. Seeing the sacrificial practice firsthand had so alarmed him that he determined to find a way to stop it:

> It is my constant prayer that there may be born on earth some great spirit, man or woman, fired with divine pity,

who will deliver us from this heinous sin, save the lives of the innocent creatures, and purify the temple.[1]

I don't think Gandhi failed to see that the agonizing longing in his own heart to save not only the sheep but his own people also was only an echo of the longing in God's heart to save all of mankind. It wasn't Jesus that had put Gandhi off Christianity. The great man very much appreciated the Christ and His teachings, as do a number of other religious and even non-religious thinkers. It was the arrogance of the Western Christians of his day which finally succeeded in putting Gandhi off Christianity.

Do you know how many Christian denominations and divisions there are in the world today? They number in the thousands, and if you count all of the major and the unaffiliated churches together, there are thousands more than these. So then, does a church membership guarantee that you are a Christian? Of course not. If you are native to the Western World, does that make you Christian? The answer seems a ridiculously simple "no" to those who live in the West, but to most of the rest of the world, this answer is often "yes." The misfortune is that the bad actions of some of us reflect on all of us and on the Christ that we follow and call others to follow. And far too many who claim the name of Jesus and say that they are Christians—simply are not.

Many will say to me in that day, Lord, Lord, have we not prophesied in thy name? and in thy name have cast out devils? and in thy name done many wonderful works?

And then will I profess unto them, I never knew you: depart from me, ye that work iniquity (Matt 7:22-23).

So then, back to the original question: How many Christian Churches are there in the world today? Answer: Seven. There are still just the same seven churches of the Revelation—and no more—regardless of the denomination or the part of the world in which they are found. And what Jesus says to the seven churches in the book of the last book of the Bible, He continues to say to us today.

To Ephesus, He says that He knows their tireless work on His behalf and their patience and endurance, but He complains that they have lost their first love for God, which is the first work of the Church. How serious is this? Serious enough to remove their lampstand from before God's throne! Love for God is the heart of the Church, and our service flows from that love. Without His beating heart, without His love, that Church will die. In fact, that Church is dead already if ever it was alive.

To Smyrna, to the suffering and persecuted Church, He has no admonition but only encouragement. He promises the crown of life to them and to all who conquer that they will not be harmed by the second death.

To Pergamum, a brutal but much-needed warning for Christians today: He warns that they had let deceptive teachers lead them into false doctrine and worldly lusts, and unless they repent, He Himself would make war against them.

To Thyatira, He has praise for many of their members but complains that they also have allowed the world, the flesh and the devil to fill them with false doctrines.

To Sardis, the dead church, He advises repentance and returning. No specific sin is mentioned beyond "soiling their clothes." It seems they simply had gone on with their religion without God. In this church, the members are very close to getting their names blotted out of the Book of Life.

To Philadelphia, remaining true to her Lord and persevering in the faith, we hear praises from Jesus.

To the Laodiceans, the church which has not been refined and not had her faith tested and proven, the wealthy and the insulated church living at ease and lulled to sleep by pride and prosperity, He warns:

> I know thy works, that thou art neither cold nor hot: I would thou wert cold or hot.
>
> So then because thou art lukewarm, and neither cold nor hot, I will spue thee out of my mouth. Because thou sayest, I am rich, and increased with goods, and have need of nothing; and knowest not that thou art wretched, and miserable, and poor, and blind, and naked (Rev 3:15-17).

There are five chastised churches in Revelation which are all self-centered, world-centered, and world-compromising churches. There are only two churches which are praised, the persecuted and the faithful churches, which are God and Heaven-centered. Unfortunately, the God-centered churches are always taking the world's blame for the actions or inactions of the other five.

Within this faithful Communion of Saints, there is manifested only one Bride of Christ eternally, the one true Church, and it is within the Wedding Supper of the Lamb that the whole of the Church becomes one in Him both in Heaven and on Earth. We are that Body of Christ which has been redeemed, washed, purified, adorned with grace by His sacrifice and filled with His Holy Spirit and with His Word. We are that tunic which Jesus wears—woven from top to bottom in one piece and without seam—this tunic which He wears next to His body, He wears next to His heart. We are His Bride. We are His Church. We are one when we are one in Him. And as we partake of the Body and Blood of His sacrifice in Holy Communion, St. Paul asks us also, "Is Christ divided?" (1 Cor 1:13).

> For as many of you as have been baptized into Christ have put on Christ.

> There is neither Jew nor Greek, there is neither bond nor free, there is neither male nor female: for ye are all one in Christ Jesus (Gal 3:27-28).

There is a way for us to deal with the barriers to our unity without losing our individual identities. Timothy Ware (the Bishop Kallistos of Diokleia) relates in his wonderful book, *The Orthodox Church*: "We Orthodox are there not simply to bear witness to what we ourselves believe, but also to listen to what others have to say."[2]

The Catechism of the Catholic Church calls other baptized Christians our separated brethren:

818 ". . . All who have been justified by faith in Baptism are incorporated into Christ; they therefore have a right to be called Christians, and with good reason are accepted as brothers in the Lord by the children of the Catholic Church."[3]

The Catechism also reflects on the unity of all believers:

814 "From the beginning, this one Church has been marked by a great diversity which comes from both the variety of God's gifts and the diversity of those who receive them."[4]

Of Protestants, there is no single Protestant Church; there are only non-Catholic, non-Orthodox churches in a Protestant or in a Reformation Movement. There is no one Protestant church and no one Reformed church which defines the doctrines or creeds that *all* the Protestant or Reformation believers must believe. (The closest thing we have to a universal declaration for all of the churches, Orthodox, Catholic, Reformed and Protestant is the Apostles Creed, and sometimes the Nicene Creed—but not all of the denominations hold to even these simple creeds and many have their own separate confessions.)

The one and only common standard that all Christians can use today through which we can begin talking to one another again is through the Divine Revelation of our Holy Bible and through the earliest of our commonly accepted creeds of belief, but it is simply astonishing how many Christians don't even have a basic understanding of either of these.

And just as Christianity has a common house with many corridors and rooms, so also, we share a common neighborhood with the rest of the Adamic race, especially with our Jewish forefathers who have developed a gentle respect for the dignity and belief (or unbelief) of others as they work to heal this fragmented, tired and often shattered old world.

This is a complex, difficult and sometimes dangerous undertaking that we assume—this healing of the world. For a while, we've been standing on the beach throwing rocks at one another, the tide has gone dramatically out to sea and a tsunami of anti-God religion has already crested and is drowning not only us but is washing away our children with its false teachings. Not content to let the wheat and the tares grow side by side until the time of the harvest (Matt: Chap 13), the tares are now insisting that the wheat must be removed from the field altogether!

As Judeo-Christianity tries to find its place at a common table with people of good will, we need to consider that there are others in these critical times who are as concerned about where we are heading as we are—and that the natural law is still written within the human heart, that law which is common to all of mankind: the law of knowing right from wrong. St. Paul confirms this:

> For when the Gentiles, which have not the law, do by nature the things contained in the law, these, having not the law, are a law unto themselves:

> Which shew the work of the law written in their hearts, their conscience also bearing witness, and their thoughts the mean while accusing or else excusing one another;

> In the day when God shall judge the secrets of men by Jesus Christ according to my gospel (Rom 2:14-16).

If Christianity is divided against Christianity, how then can we ever expect to talk to the rest of the world? And if Christianity stays divided against Christianity, then from a place of weakness and confusion of voices, we will be forced (and even now are being forced) to accept any alternative that the world imposes upon us.

> And I, brethren, could not speak unto you as unto spiritual, but as unto carnal, even as unto babes in Christ. I have fed you with milk, and not with meat: for hitherto ye were not able to bear it, neither yet now are ye able. For ye are yet carnal: for whereas there is among you envying, and strife, and divisions, are ye not carnal, and walk as men?

> For while one saith, I am of Paul; and another, I am of Apollos; are ye not carnal? (1 Cor 3:1-4).

7

LAW AND GRACE

THESIS, ANTITHESIS, AND SYNTHESIS; TYPE, ANTITYPE, AND SUPERSESSIONISM

Here are six terms and their definitions that are essential to answering the question of Christian primacy: Thesis, Antithesis, and Synthesis; Type and Antitype, and Supersessionism.

Thesis, antithesis and synthesis are the three most exacting words I can think of to begin this chapter which covers a number of hard questions that Christians often ask. The thesis, in this case, would be the Old Testament witness to law, justice, retribution and punishment. The antithesis to that would be the New Testament gifts of grace, mercy, forgiveness and freedom. These are the bookends of the Bible. Synthesis is when these two are joined together as one by Christ's sacrificial death, burial and resurrection on our behalf to pay the price of which that justice requires of us. Israel was chosen not only to bear witness to God's voice in Old Testament truths but to document, protect and preserve those truths throughout all of the countless failings of mankind's history.

Without law and justice (Old Testament), grace and mercy (New Testament) have no meaning.

Type and Antitype can also be words associated with contrasting or opposite types, but used in association with the Bible, again as a whole, it means that the laws and prophecies entrusted to Judaism to protect and to live out in the Old Covenant are fulfilled perfectly by Jesus Christ in the New Covenant. The Old Covenant is the type, the prefigurement or foreshadowing of the New Covenant, which is its antitype—the completion and satisfaction of the demands of that type. In this, Jews (Old Testament) and Christians (New Testament) together give body, soul and spirit to the hope of all mankind. Don't let the *anti* in antitype confuse you: here, it means the final consummation of the type.

The Christian Pentecostal celebration of the Holy Spirit being poured out upon believers happened, not coincidently, on the Jewish festival celebration of Shavuot (Pentecost), which celebrates the Torah and the Law being given to Moses on Mount Sinai: neither Grace vs. Law, nor Grace doing away with Law, but Grace perfectly fulfilling the requirements of the Law in a way that natural man cannot do. Only when law and justice are known and understood do mercy and grace seem so much the greater. Adam dies for disobedience, but Christ lives again in perfect obedience— and through Him and by the grace of God, so do we. As we die to the old Adam, we are resurrected in the new Adam. The Christ of

God takes upon Himself the death sentence for what is broken in our obedience to the Law, but He does not, in any way, do away with the requirement for it. It is not an either/or.

Let nothing and no one ever separate Law from Grace or Grace from Law! Or Judeo from Christianity. Or the Old Testament from the New Testament. And certainly, never let anyone ever convince you that you are exempt from the Law because Grace has replaced it.

Without the authority of God's laws, creation descends into the waters of primordial chaos again. Without the authority of God's laws for the order of mankind, we descend also but into a darkness that is far greater than those primordial waters—a void so complete and so deep that no light can ever enter into it and nothing can ever escape it. When you take Christ off the Cross and say that it is all about "love, love, love, forget the Law," you are no longer Christian. Without the sacrifice of Christ, you are not saved from your sins and the penalty for those sins.

Become still for just a moment. Now try to imagine the enormous cost that Jesus had to pay in order to buy you back from the darkness of that void. Read the next two quotes and then read them again.

> Depart from evil, and do good; and dwell for evermore. For the Lord loveth judgment, and forsaketh not his saints; they are preserved for ever: but the seed of the wicked shall be cut off (Ps 37: 27-28).

> Now from the sixth hour there was darkness over all the land unto the ninth hour.
>
> And about the ninth hour Jesus cried with a loud voice, saying, Eli, Eli, lama sabachthani? that is to say, My God, my God, why hast thou forsaken me? (Matt 27:45-46).

Erase for a moment all of the preconceived notions of hell that you have in mind. First and foremost, hell is separation from God and the good of all His Creation. There is no light there and no time there. It is a total emptiness and it is forever. It is a place of utter self-absorption where you are limited to the senseless chattering of your own soul's thoughts forevermore. It lies even beyond the primordial waters of chaos. *It is a constant awareness of nothingness. It is an unquenched thirsting for somethingness, for life.* You were created a living and eternal soul by the breath of the eternal and living God. But when you chose to be separated from your Creator, you chose to be separated from His Creation also. There is no greater fire that burns than this complete isolation, and the greatest terror of hell is the loss of all hope—this is your final and forever destination: "but the seed of the wicked shall be cut off" (Ps 37: 28).

This is very important, so please read it carefully: Beyond the torture of the Cross, Jesus, the Christ of God, descended into hell for us and only the Son of God could have resurrected from there. It is a serious sin to think of your salvation from hell and its eternal consequences as a superficial right which is tagged on to your

Halleluiah chorus. Your salvation is not free from cost. And when you change one word of Scripture, you can change a whole lot. When you change one word of the ancient creeds, you change their whole meaning. Jesus, our Savior, descended into hell—for us. "My God, my God, why hast thou forsaken me?" (Matt 27:46).

Consider again, what good would it be for Christians to preach forgiveness of sins to a world that has no law but the law which it creates for itself? As we carry the Cross of Christ's mercy into the world, we must always remember that Israel has already gone before us carrying the Ark of the Covenant. But if you believe that you have inherited and assumed all that belongs to Israel's Covenant with God, then you are indebted to do the whole of that Covenant and everything that is written within that Covenant's 613 commandments and ordinances.

The Son of God chose to be born into the Jewish nation of Israel, that nation to whom the Written Law was entrusted, that He might fulfill the righteousness of which that Law requires of us— fulfill it in our place—by taking upon Himself our judgment for breaking it, even all the way to Hell.

Do you know the meaning of Israel's Ark of the Old Covenant and what it carried within it as it is found in the New Testament? And what overshadowed its mercy seat? You should.

And after the second veil, the tabernacle which is called the Holiest of all;

> Which had the golden censer, and the ark of the covenant
> overlaid round about with gold, wherein was the golden pot
> that had manna, and Aaron's rod that budded, and the tables
> of the covenant;
>
> And over it the cherubims of glory shadowing the
> mercyseat; of which we cannot now speak particularly (Heb
> 9:3-5).

In many Christian traditions, Mary is called the Ark of the New
Covenant because of what she carried within her: the manna of the
Last Supper, this is My Body, this is My Blood (our Holy
Communion); the rod that resurrected to life again to become the
Tree of Life for us in the New Jerusalem (Christ's cross and His
resurrection from the dead); and the fulfillment of the
righteousness of the tablet of the Law (Christ Himself). All of
these are embodied, incarnated, in the Child she carried within
her—the Christ Child—as Mary becomes the Ark of the New
Covenant who sheltered her Divine Son. And the "cherubims of
glory shadowing the mercy seat"?

> And suddenly there was with the angel a multitude of the
> heavenly host praising God, and saying, Glory to God in the
> highest, and on earth peace, good will toward men" (Luke
> 2:13-14).

Other words, such as continuity, consistency, coherence and
seamlessness forever link the Jewish and Christian narratives
together. God's work is the work of creation, but it is also a work

of re-creation. Miraculously, faithful Israel remains to this day in spite of the intolerable efforts that have been carried out to exterminate her during the whole of her existence—endures with all of her Law protected and intact—because God loves Israel with a depth of love that we cannot begin to fathom. For the sake of the fathers, their calling is irrevocable, and God's mercy is everlasting to them.

Consider Adam, to whom the first promise of redemption was made. And what of Noah, who "found grace in the eyes of the Lord" (Gen 6:8). And what of Father Abraham? What of Moses to whom the written law was given—and the prophets to whom the Word of the Lord came? What of David who, when "Samuel anointed him in the midst of his brethren . . . the Spirit of the Lord came upon David from that day forward" (1 Sam 16:13)—of whom Jesus declared, "I am the root and the offspring of David, and the bright and morning star" (Rev 22:16). Were these not chosen? St. Paul writes to the Romans:

> Who are Israelites; to whom pertaineth the adoption, and the glory, and the covenants, and the giving of the law, and the service of God, and the promises;
>
> Whose are the fathers, and of whom as concerning the flesh Christ came, who is over all, God blessed for ever. Amen (Rom 9:4-5).

And yet, if only through the Sacrifice of Christ are we saved, how does this reconcile with faithful Israel being saved at the time of the end of the Gentiles? And not just Israel, but it seems the whole world is looking for her Messiah, a long-ago prophesied Deliverer Who will restore a new world to peace and safety and righteousness once more—in every culture and in every tongue, the longed-for Heavenly Messiah. He Who was promised to our first parents: Adam, male and female, created He them.

Here is one of the greatest of the mysteries of God. When Messiah appears, when the King of Peace and Righteousness comes, when our eternal High Priest is revealed ("You are a priest forever, according to the order of Melchizedek"), does He, Who is the fulfillment of the office of Melchizedek, in direct decent from Noah and from Adam (without lineage from the Levitical priesthood), will He not come once again to faithful Abram to whom God promised: "Neither shall thy name any more be called Abram, but thy name shall be Abraham; for a father of many nations have I made thee" (Gen 17:5). Is this not only the fulfillment of the Old Covenant prophecies but also of St. Paul's New Covenant prophecy for the final salvation of Israel? And Jesus, Prophet and King and both the High Priest and the Sacrifice offered for our sins—does He not come to Abraham once more with His offering of the Bread and the Wine of mankind's redemption, as Melchizedek prophesied? "This is My Body. This is My Blood."

For I would not, brethren, that ye should be ignorant of this mystery, lest ye should be wise in your own conceits; that blindness in part is happened to Israel, until the fulness of the Gentiles be come in.

And so all Israel shall be saved: as it is written, There shall come out of Sion the Deliverer, and shall turn away ungodliness from Jacob:

For this is my covenant unto them, when I shall take away their sins (Rom 11:25-27).

So finally, we come to the final word of this chapter: Supersessionism. Does Christianity supersede Judaism? Are we the New Israel? Or are there two intimately related covenants with God, both still valid, the old and the new, which are finally consummated into one when Messiah returns? Are the Two Witnesses recorded in the book of Revelation at the end of time, Law and Grace: the Old Covenant of Justice and the New Covenant of Mercy?

"And I will give power unto my two witnesses, and they shall prophesy a thousand two hundred and threescore days, clothed in sackcloth" (Rev 11:3).

Whose names were written in the Book of Life before the foundation of the world? Before Adam? Before Abraham? Before David? Before Jesus, the Son of God, the Word made flesh, was born into the world of time that He created—whose names were written forever in God's Book of Life?

And what about the righteousness of those who obey only the natural law written in their hearts from the beginning of the Creation but have never even heard of Jesus or Moses or Abraham or even of Adam? What about the righteous who were born before the Age of Christianity? Or before Abraham was born? Or before Moses wrote down the Law? Or what about that righteous young man in the deepest darkest jungle who obeys the Adamic natural law written deep within his heart, who looks to the heavens with longing in his soul, surrounded only by the call of the Holy Spirit to that which he does not understand but to Whom he answers— this young man that everyone has been worrying about for centuries, but who has never even heard of any of this? St. Paul writes after Christ was crucified and after Christ was resurrected and ascended:

> For as many as have sinned without law shall also perish without law: and as many as have sinned in the law shall be judged by the law; (For not the hearers of the law are just before God, but the doers of the law shall be justified.
>
> For when the Gentiles, which have not the law, do by nature the things contained in the law, these, having not the law, are a law unto themselves:
>
> Which shew the work of the law written in their hearts, their conscience also bearing witness, and their thoughts the mean while accusing or else excusing one another;)

In the day when God shall judge the secrets of men by Jesus Christ according to my gospel (Rom 2:12-16).

And again, Paul says:

For he is not a Jew, which is one outwardly; neither is that circumcision, which is outward in the flesh: But he is a Jew, which is one inwardly; and circumcision is that of the heart, in the spirit, and not in the letter; whose praise is not of men, but of God (Rom 2:28-29).

So then, what about these others? Christians are a minority in a world which is filled with others; and many are 'others,' but not by their own choice.

For now, Christians know only our path, the path that Christians must travel as we continue to witness not only to the Grace of God but to the Law of God, which only that Grace can satisfy. Of the many great and deep mysteries of which God has chosen not to entrust to us, Jesus simply tells us, ". . . follow thou me." This is not just Peter inquiring about John's path in life, but it is our inquiring about our own path in life. Jesus says to us also, "If I will that he tarry till I come, what is that to thee? follow thou me" (John 21:22).

Here is the final question for Christians then: When our long-awaited Bridegroom finally returns, will He find His Bride keeping a faithful watch over His household? While she waits for His return, will she continue to carry on His work of healing Adam and of healing the world? Will she be found still proclaiming His Name and His Sacrifice for the nations, to the nations?

Or will the Son of God return to find His Beloved Bride sleeping with His enemy—and beating up on her fellow servants?

SECTION III

MANIFESTING THE TRINITY

Thou hast set our iniquities before thee, our secret sins in the light of thy countenance.

For all our days are passed away in thy wrath: we spend our years as a tale that is told (Ps 90: 8-9).

8

THE SIMPLICITY OF GOD

TRANSCENDENT, (IN) COMPREHENSIBLE, (UN)KNOWABLE, (IN)VISIBLE

It is not the complexity of God that we don't understand. It is His utter simplicity. God's perfection lies in His simplicity. He is not perfect. He is Perfection. Nothing can be added to God and nothing taken away. He is not an amalgamate of personalities or a combination of attributes and qualities. He is One and He is the Fountainhead of all that is. Those things which we attribute to God, such as truth, mercy, love, goodness and creative force, even the wrath of God, which is a demonstration of the justice of God, are not in God as they are in us—they are God Nothing can hold, contain, surround, penetrate or add to the essence of God. He is not in eternity; He is Eternity as He is Infinity. He is whole. He is complete. He is unchanging, immutable. He is pure, uncorrupted and unmixed simplicity. He is One and He is Holy.

Peter Kreeft explains: "God does not fall in love for the same reason that water does not get wet."[1] Therefore, we can confidently say that God is Love.

God must constantly give of Himself to make His Existence, the only existence, that is, our existence. God is that necessary Being Who makes our being possible. "And God said unto Moses, I Am That I Am: and he said, Thus shalt thou say unto the children of Israel, I Am hath sent me unto you" (Ex 3:14).

Contrast the God of the Bible with an old heresy which is evident in the religion of the New Age Pantheism of today, wherein god is a "force," and we, and all of nature, are only manifestations of that force—even to the extent that all and everything in the universe is god. This has resurrected as a popular theme in the entertainment industries and denies the existence of the personhood of God Himself, as well as the Creator of His (showing ownership) Creation. Pantheism is devoid of ownership, of reason, of an intelligent design or an absolute authority—and thus morality and accountability. To what would you be accountable? There is no Supreme Being in pantheism, no LORD of all to whom we can appeal. No Whom at all if everything is god. In the coldness of the pantheistic world, there is no god who can love us or even judge us. There is no Who—there is only a 'what.'

So how can we measure the immeasurable, calculate the incalculable, and understand the absolute uncorrupted simplicity of

God?   How can we more name Existence than God names Himself: "I AM." How does dust measure Eternity? By what law does mortality judge Immortality, ignorance challenge Omniscience, powerlessness defy Omnipotence?   And how can our corruption come into the presence of the absolute, the pure and the just, "I AM."   God can be no other than the "I AM" of His declared Being.

Yet, this same transcendent, incomprehensible, unknowable and invisible God, incredibly, bids us call Him "Father." What a great and unthinkable tragedy it is to refuse Him. What an immense loss it is not to know the God who made us in His Image so that we *can* know Him—and by this knowing, come to love Him—this God, Who assures us that we are known and loved by Him.

Transcendent and beyond us always, yes, but through the incarnation, through the en-fleshment of His Son, God suddenly becomes personal, comprehensible, knowable, and yes, even visible. The Father reveals Himself in the Son.

> Jesus saith unto him, Have I been so long time with you, and yet hast thou not known me, Philip? he that hath seen me hath seen the Father; and how sayest thou then, Show us the Father? (John 14:9).

A transcendent Creator means that there is a transcendental quality in the lives of those who are not only created in His image but are brought to life with His very breath. We are creatures made wholly natural; and yet, at the same time, made wholly supranatural (above nature). We are also preternatural, made of the natural world but inherently able to live beyond our natural earthly existence. God gives us a natural, supranatural and preternatural living soul when He breathes His Life into us. That is why our creation can only be completed in Him. I was created; I am being created, and I will be created when the life of the Holy Spirit is fully realized in me. We are back to Genesis again:

> And the Lord God formed man of the dust of the ground, and breathed into his nostrils the breath of life; and man became a living soul (Gen 2:7).

This is important. To lose sight of this singular answer to life's complex questions is to lose sight of the miraculous reason of why we should exist at all. The Christ of God did not become one of us, but He did miraculously make Himself one with us, remaining wholly Divine while at the same time becoming completely human. God incarnate, not only walking in our flesh but immersing Himself into all that makes us human, yet without sin. And the Christ of God did not become one with us in order to bring His Divinity into our humanity; He became one with us in order to raise our humanity into His Divinity.

> Now all this was done, that it might be fulfilled which was spoken of the Lord by the prophet, saying,
>
> Behold, a virgin shall be with child, and shall bring forth a son, and they shall call his name Emmanuel, which being

interpreted is, God with us (Matt 1:22-23 referring to Is 7:14).

Even little children could now behold the Face of God: Jesus, the Christ of God, the promised Messiah.

> Then were there brought unto him little children, that he should put his hands on them, and pray: and the disciples rebuked them.

> But Jesus said, Suffer little children, and forbid them not, to come unto me: for of such is the kingdom of heaven (Matt 19:13-14).

Jesus becomes for us the transcendent, yet approachable and touchable, Son of God— "God from God, Light from Light, true God from true God," says the Nicene Creed—Jesus, the Word of God, the One Who made all things was born into His own Creation, born of a Virgin.

> No man hath seen God at any time, the only begotten Son, which is in the bosom of the Father, he hath declared him (John 1:18).

> Believest thou not that I am in the Father, and the Father in me? the words that I speak unto you I speak not of myself: but the Father that dwelleth in me, he doeth the works (John 14:10).

The Reverends John Trigilio and Kenneth Brighenti, in their Catholicism Answer Book, demonstrate the Trinity of God in the understanding of two very different math equations.[2]

The Trinity is not: $1 + 1 + 1 = 3$

The Trinity is: $1 \times 1 \times 1 = 1$

In other words, there are three distinct persons but only one Divine Essence, one Divine Nature, one Divine Mind, and one Divine Will. There is only One God. Jesus says, "If I have told you earthly things, and ye believe not, how shall ye believe, if I tell you of heavenly things? (John 3:12).

When Jesus was baptized, He Who was without sin willingly immersed Himself into the sins of all mankind; and when He arose from His Baptismal waters, He came forth carrying those sins upon Himself. Thus are the waters of our own baptism cleansed and purified with His perfect sinlessness. The Father tells the alienated and suffering race of Adam in a voice from Heaven, "This is my beloved Son, in whom I am well pleased" (Matt 3:17). And just as He hovered above the primordial waters at the First Creation, God's Holy Spirit descends upon the New Creation as Jesus is driven into our wilderness of temptation, suffering and death. For Jesus, the Christ of God, His Baptism was where He picked up our sins on His walk to Calvary.

By faith, Christians know that when we physically and mystically pass through these purified baptismal waters and receive the anointing of the Holy Spirit when we arise from them, we will then follow Jesus, the Christ of God, the Word of God, into our own wilderness to be tested and tried until our faith and trust in God is purified and we are strengthened. We must not only be renewed, but we must be wholly regenerated and transformed so that we can follow the Son back into the world again. Our Baptism is our own spiritual death, burial and resurrection as we are reborn into a new life in Christ: and as we are baptized into His death, so are we also resurrected into the newness of His own resurrected life.

For he hath made him to be sin for us, who knew no sin; that we might be made the righteousness of God in him (2 Cor 5: 21).

If the first prayer of mankind to God is, "Who are You anyway?" our second prayer should be "My Lord and My God!" as He reveals Himself evermore clearly to us in answer to that prayer. What else is possible but to make our own act of submission and complete and final offering of our will to the will of God? "Here am I, Lord."

I had a free lunch hour one day, which I used to slip into a pew in the downtown Cathedral. All kinds of people came to worship and pray that day, and one by one they left again until the church was finally empty (or at least I thought it was empty). That was when I began to hear the first notes of the most exquisite song that I had ever heard. It was coming, ever so quietly and softly, from a young woman who was in rapt adoration before the altar. So beautiful was her song that I thought she must be a vision of an angel who had come to worship with us that day. This young woman, who was privately pouring out her love before God, in her perfect voice, in her perfect song, in an extraordinary offering of herself to Him in this intimate sacrifice of private adoration, made me realize that all my years of careful studying were as nothing in her presence. "Here am I, Lord. Lord, it is only here that I truly, truly am." To which He always responds, "Be still, and know that I am God" (Ps 46:10).

It is for the fullness of joy that we were created—but how can God give that which will not be received? And how can He fill that which will not be offered to Him? Truly, the unforgivable sin against the Holy Spirit is to refuse Him.

> Thus saith the Lord, Stand ye in the ways, and see, and ask for the old paths, where is the good way, and walk therein, and ye shall find rest for your souls. But they said, We will not walk therein (Jer 6:16).

9

THE HOLINESS OF GOD

PRAYER

Christians want to be good. God wants us to be holy. Christians want their prayers answered. God wants to pour His life into us. Christians want to be saved from the fires of Hell. But God wants more than our justification—He wants our sanctification. He wants to complete the work that He has begun in us. He wants to bring us into the fullness of life with the breath of His Holy Spirit. This is Sanctifying Grace and we receive the completeness of it when we come into the Divine Presence and freely accept that which is being poured out upon us and into us.

> Beloved, now are we the sons of God, and it doth not yet appear what we shall be: but we know that, when he shall appear, we shall be like him; for we shall see him as he is (1 John 3:2).

As Christianity continues to grow-up into Christ, and as we struggle to fully become what we were created to be, we come to a place beyond the justification of our salvation and into the sanctification of a Holy union with our Creator. And as we rethink self-examination, confession and the purging of all that keeps us from being fully present to a Holy God, we come to realize how utterly unworthy we are of this great honor of praying—and yet, still, He summons us, "Come unto Me."

The Jesus Prayer of Orthodoxy permeates and saturates the Orthodox soul: "Lord Jesus Christ, Son of God, have mercy on me, a sinner." Even Moses was warned not to come too close and to take off his shoes, for the ground upon which he was standing was Holy Ground (Ex 3:5). So, here is something else to remember before you pray: *All prayer is standing on Holy Ground.*

> And the publican, standing afar off, would not lift up so much as his eyes unto heaven, but smote upon his breast, saying, God be merciful to me a sinner (Luke 18:13).

The very best of prayers is when we stand silently before God in this nakedness of soul and make a sacrificial offering of ourselves to His will: "Here am I, Lord."

> And the angel of the Lord called unto him out of heaven, and said, Abraham, Abraham: and he said, Here am I (Gen 22:11).

> And when the Lord saw that he turned aside to see, God called unto him out of the midst of the bush, and said, Moses, Moses. And he said, Here am I (Ex 3:4).

The Lord called Samuel: and he answered, Here am I (1 Sam 3:4).

Then said I, Woe is me! for I am undone; because I am a man of unclean lips, and I dwell in the midst of a people of unclean lips: for mine eyes have seen the King, the Lord of hosts.

Then flew one of the seraphims unto me, having a live coal in his hand, which he had taken with the tongs from off the altar:

And he laid it upon my mouth, and said, Lo, this hath touched thy lips; and thine iniquity is taken away, and thy sin purged.

Also I heard the voice of the Lord, saying, Whom shall I send, and who will go for us? Then said I, Here am I; send me (Isa 6:5-8).

The book of Revelation begins with a call to repentance and confession. Even the Lord's Prayer has a petition for the forgiveness of our own sins as we pray for the forgiveness of others. So how, and when, and why did we lose our fear of the Lord?

The fear of the Lord is the beginning of knowledge: but fools despise wisdom and instruction" (Prov 1:7).

By mercy and truth iniquity is purged: and by the fear of the Lord men depart from evil (Prov 16:6).

This is so important that we should further define sin:

> *Anything that separates you from God and from His will for*
> *you is sin.*

Thomas Merton takes this subject even further: (Sin is) ". . . our refusal to be what we were created to be—sons of God, images of God."[1] Merton then drives home his point: "It is not sufficient for the tree to remain alive, it must also bear fruit."[2] This was in explanation of a quote from St. John Chrysostom's Homily xvi on Ephesians: "It is not enough to leave Egypt; one must also travel to the Promised Land." [3]

If justification comes to us through the sacrifice and resurrection of the Christ of God, and our baptism is the washing away of those sins which separate us from God, then our sanctification must be something that we acquire on our long journey to the Promised Land.

> And the Lord went before them by day in a pillar of a cloud,
> to lead them the way; and by night in a pillar of fire, to give
> them light; to go by day and night (Ex 13:21).

A man named Nicholas Herman became Brother Lawrence in the mid-17th century in Paris when he consecrated his life to God and went into a Monastery. His little book, *The Practice of the Presence of God*, has become a prayer manual for countless generations and is still in print. When asked to describe his prayer life to others, he wrote:

I consider myself as the most wretched of men, full of sores and corruption, and who has committed all sorts of crimes against his King. Touched with a sensible regret, I confess to Him all my wickedness. I ask His forgiveness. I abandon myself in His hands that He may do what He pleases with me. The King, full of mercy and goodness, very far from chastising me, embraces me with love, makes me eat at His table, serves me with His own hands, gives me the key of His treasures; He converses and delights Himself with me incessantly, in a thousand and a thousand ways, and treats me in all respects as His favorite.[4]

C. S. Lewis goes even further into the life of prayer when he describes the necessity of our 'hatching', of our need to allow God to pour His transforming grace into us so that He can cleanse us and complete His Image in us. In Mere Christianity, Lewis explains:

"It may be hard for an egg to turn into a bird: it would be a jolly sight harder for it to learn to fly while remaining an egg. We are like eggs at present. And you cannot go on indefinitely being just an ordinary, decent egg. We must be hatched or go bad."[5]

Prayer is surrendering again and again to the Potter's wheel so that He can make something beautiful of us: modeling, firing, cooling, glazing and firing again. But prayer is even more wonderfully terrifying than being made ready to stand on Holy

Ground; for within the stillness of our now quieted hearts and minds, and with the final and complete surrender of all that is ours to give, we now find ourselves barefoot and naked before our Maker—humbled and trembling before the burning bush which cleanses but does not devour. "Here am I Lord. It is only here that I truly, truly am."

It amazes me that so many of us just don't want to be here, in this place, before the burning bush. "Thus far and no farther shall you come Lord", Christians say, "I thank you kindly, but I'll do this my way."

God never at any time violates your reason or your free will— but He will never settle for a second best in us either.

THE MOST IMPORTANT ADDENDUM TO PRAYER:
Nevertheless

But now that we are made ready to petition God with our prayers, we have reached a Scriptural conundrum: a riddle, a puzzle, a mystery that is imbedded in our instructions for praying: *How do we pray the believers' prayer and stand firm by anticipating the answers to our requests—and at the same time be willing to accept God's rejection of that request or an answer that is in opposition to that request?*

And he went a little farther, and fell on his face, and prayed, saying, O my Father, if it be possible, let this cup pass from me: nevertheless not as I will, but as thou wilt (Matt 26:42).

Sometimes the mountain that we are praying to have removed is in God's plans for us and must be accepted. Sometimes the mountain itself is the answer to the prayer, even if it is sitting right on top of us. We pray fervently for it to be removed, and by God's grace, and when the reason for its existence is fulfilled, *it will move*. We can move mountains with our prayers—but only in God's way, in God's time, and under the supervision of God's understanding of the greater things that He has in mind for us, do we ask for it to be moved: *nevertheless*.

Jesus drank from the cup of His Father's will; on the third day He was raised again and now He reigns in glory. Jesus not only moved mountains with His prayers, but because of His perfect obedience and submission to His Father's will, He also moved both Heaven and Earth when He added, "nevertheless", and "thy will be done".

Now there is just one more thing to be done before you pray, and perhaps it will be the hardest challenge you will ever face in this life—so you will need the power of the Third Person of the Holy Trinity to accomplish it: 1 x 1 x 1 = 1. You are asked to forgive.

> And when ye stand praying, forgive, if ye have ought against any: that your Father also which is in heaven may forgive you your trespasses (Mark 11:25).

COME, HOLY SPIRIT

RENEWING THE FACE OF THE EARTH

The Holy Spirit is described as the Breath of God, as the Finger of God, as the Wind and the Fire, the Wisdom and the Love of God. He is called Counselor, Comforter, Healer, Teacher, and Guide. He gives us the courage and the gifts to be and to do in God's Holy Name. Blessed with the riches of His Presence, mankind becomes endowed with the full spectrum of God's good life. He is worshipped and glorified together with the Father and the Son. He is God. He is the Third Person of the Holy Trinity: $1 \times 1 \times 1 = 1$.

> Therefore if any man be in Christ, he is a new creature: old things are passed away; behold, all things are become new (2 Cor 5:17).

The Holy Spirit personally summons each one of us home, and one by one we come. The Holy Spirit binds us to Christ and to one another, thereby forming within Himself the one true Body of

Christ in Heaven and on earth. The Holy Spirit is the Soul of the Church. It is through Him that we are called, through Scripture, through the sacrifice of the Son of God and through our own baptism in the name of the Holy Trinity (Father, Son and Holy Spirit) that we find our common Christian unity. Christ makes visible the invisible God to the world and calls us to do the same. The Holy Spirit fills us with sanctifying grace which enables us to carry out the work of Christ in this world. He is ever present, ever working in us, and forever revealing God's presence to us.

> But ye shall receive power, after that the Holy Ghost is come upon you: and ye shall be witnesses unto me both in Jerusalem, and in all Judaea, and in Samaria, and unto the uttermost part of the earth (Acts 1:8).

> Wherefore I give you to understand, that no man speaking by the Spirit of God calleth Jesus accursed: and that no man can say that Jesus is the Lord, but by the Holy Ghost.

> Now there are diversities of gifts, but the same Spirit.

> And there are differences of administrations, but the same Lord.

> And there are diversities of operations, but it is the same God which worketh all in all.

> But the manifestation of the Spirit is given to every man to profit withal (I Cor 12:3-7).

The Apostle Paul's Trinitarian Benediction to the Corinthians is a perfect revelation of the Holy Trinity working in behalf of the Body of Christ through grace, love and communion, "The grace of the Lord Jesus Christ, and the love of God, and the communion of the Holy Ghost, be with you all. Amen" (2 Cor 13:14).

Here we also find the order of our response to God: to know, to love and to serve Him. "Holy, Holy, Holy," declare the angels before the throne of God: 1 x 1 x 1 = 1.

> And one cried unto another, and said, Holy, holy, holy, is the Lord of hosts: the whole earth is full of his glory (Isa 6:3).

> And the four beasts had each of them six wings about him; and they were full of eyes within: and they rest not day and night, saying, Holy, holy, holy, Lord God Almighty, which was, and is, and is to come (Rev 4:8).

It is a well-meaning phrase (and even Biblical) when someone comes to you in your time of great trouble and says, "God will not ask of you more than you are able." As anyone who has been there can tell you, "Oh yes He does!" He does ask more of us than we are naturally able in order to stretch and expand and mature the depth of our faith in Him. "More than we are able" brings us to the point of Job's sweet surrender—to the place where the Holy Spirit can finally and fully perfect His work within us.

> And he said unto me, My grace is sufficient for thee: for my strength is made perfect in weakness. Most gladly therefore will I rather glory in my infirmities, that the power of Christ may rest upon me.
>
> Therefore I take pleasure in infirmities, in reproaches, in necessities, in persecutions, in distresses for Christ's sake: for when I am weak, then am I strong (2 Cor 12:9-10).

In every language, and all together, Christians should be praying: *"Lord, send out your Spirit and renew the face of the earth."*

> Again he said unto me, Prophesy upon these bones, and say unto them, O ye dry bones, hear the word of the Lord.
>
> Thus saith the Lord God unto these bones; Behold, I will cause breath to enter into you, and ye shall live (Ezek 37:4-5).

"Lord, send out your Spirit and renew the face of the earth."

> And it shall come to pass afterward, that I will pour out my spirit upon all flesh; and your sons and your daughters shall prophesy, your old men shall dream dreams, your young men shall see visions:
>
> And also upon the servants and upon the handmaids in those days will I pour out my spirit (Joel 2:28-29).

The Word of God, the Breath of God, the Hand of Christ in ours, and the Blessing of the Father upon us enables us to see and, therefore, to cry out in true worship: *Abba! Father!*

> And there shall come forth a rod out of the stem of Jesse, and a Branch shall grow out of his roots:
>
> And the spirit of the Lord shall rest upon him, the spirit of wisdom and understanding, the spirit of counsel and might, the spirit of knowledge and of the fear of the Lord (Isa 11:1-2).

"Lord, send out your Spirit and renew the face of the earth."

Those without hope are children who have been taught that there is no God. "You're an animal, so act like one!" Ironically, this same society which robs our children of God has graphically taught them to believe in demons and devils!

Where are you on God's line of created time? How late is it getting to be? We are living during a period of great revival but also in a time of great darkness, apostasy—and danger.

"Lord, send out your Spirit and renew the face of the earth!"

> And when the day of Pentecost was fully come, they were all with one accord in one place.
>
> And suddenly there came a sound from heaven as of a rushing mighty wind, and it filled all the house where they were sitting.

And there appeared unto them cloven tongues like as of fire, and it sat upon each of them.

And they were all filled with the Holy Ghost, and began to speak with other tongues, as the Spirit gave them utterance (Acts 2:1-4).

"Lord, send out your Spirit and renew the face of the earth!"

SECTION IV:

THE END IS THE BEGINNING

The days of our years are threescore years and ten; and if by reason of strength they be fourscore years, yet is their strength labour and sorrow; for it is soon cut off, and we fly away.

Who knoweth the power of thine anger? even according to thy fear, so is thy wrath.

So teach us to number our days, that we may apply our hearts unto wisdom (Ps 90: 10-12).

THE NUMBERING OF OUR DAYS

JUDE'S PRELUDE TO JOHN'S SONG

We worship. We pray. We work. We witness. We wait in great anticipation. And yes, we suffer. Yet, there still lies before us one more Passover night's watch before the return of the Lord in judgment—and if the Church will not purge itself, then God will purge her for us. As we watch the world darkening around us once more, we may well see the full measure of those who are being saved in our own generations while simultaneously having to withstand the growing "mystery of iniquity" as it takes unprecedented power over the world again.

> "For the mystery of iniquity doth already work: only he who now letteth will let, until he be taken out of the way" (2 Thess 2:7).

During the Season of Advent, we meditate on the two major events of our Christian faith which define the Reign of Christ within His Church in time:

1. First, we meditate on the Second Coming of the Christ, which will finally make known to mankind the fierce judgment of God on those who have *refused* Him and His authority and His mercy and His love (the unforgivable sin).

But for those who have accepted Him:

> For since the beginning of the world men have not heard, nor perceived by the ear, neither hath the eye seen, O God, beside thee, what he hath prepared for him that waiteth for him (Is 64:4).

> But as it is written, Eye hath not seen, nor ear heard, neither have entered into the heart of man, the things which God hath prepared for them that love him (1 Cor 2:9)

2. Second, we meditate on the First Coming of the Christ in the Incarnation, which culminates in the Season of Christmas—the season which flows from and follows Advent. Our understanding of what *will* happen at the end of the age significantly enhances our appreciation of what *did* happen in the Incarnation. Between these two events lies the whole of the Christian life on earth, which is the Age of the Church. Christ remains with us always in this Age, through our Holy Communion, but also through something that C. S. Lewis called *Numinous Christianity*—an all-consuming

awareness of God's Presence and a certain fearful and wondrous awe and longing for Him. This is where we come to understand why anything that separates us from that Presence is death for us and for our world, and that which He provides for us to come back to Him, the author of Life, again and again, is not only our redemption but life itself, even while we are still here on earth. The Holy Spirit calls to every soul, but how few *truly* answer.

The Revelation of John comes after Jude's final warnings. Read correctly. It is a summation of our faith which culminates in the Marriage Feast of the Lamb. It is rich in meaning for us. It opens the door of our understanding. It is so necessary to our faith that it is imperative that we stand next to John and simply let him explain to us the meaning of what he sees from the same place where he sees it. No private interpretation of it can ever be made. Much like the Book of Genesis, simply believe that what is written is true and you can see it too.

The Book of Jude is included here as *the last book of the Bible.* It issues a final warning to the Church to repent and to return to God before that great day when Christ will return for His Bride. The following quotation from the little book of Jude is presented here not as its own chapter but as the final chapter, the final book of the New Testament, which acts as the bridge to John's triumphant song in Revelation. Jude is a warning to the Church on a number of issues that we are facing today. It is significant that the last book of the New Testament concludes the New Testament narrative with a Church in disarray. Revelation is a book unto itself, but it picks up just where Jude leaves off—with a now glorified Christ issuing final warnings to these same Churches. Jude is the theme of Advent, which is a warning of the judgment to come while still offering mercy and blessing to those who will repent and return.

Once saved, always saved? Not according to Jude.

> I will therefore put you in remembrance, though ye once knew this, how that the Lord, having saved the people out of the land of Egypt, afterward destroyed them that believed not.

> And the angels which kept not their first estate, but left their own habitation, he hath reserved in everlasting chains under darkness unto the judgment of the great day.

> Even as Sodom and Gomorrah, and the cities about them in like manner, giving themselves over to fornication, and going after strange flesh, are set forth for an example, suffering the vengeance of eternal fire.

> Likewise also, these filthy dreamers defile the flesh, despise dominion, and speak evil of dignities.

> Yet Michael the archangel, when contending with the devil he disputed about the body of Moses, durst not bring against him a railing accusation, but said, The Lord rebuke thee.

But these speak evil of those things which they know not: but what they know naturally, as brute beasts, in those things they corrupt themselves.

Woe unto them! for they have gone in the way of Cain, and ran greedily after the error of Balaam for reward, and perished in the gainsaying of Core.

These are spots in your feasts of charity, when they feast with you, feeding themselves without fear: clouds they are without water, carried about of winds; trees whose fruit withereth, without fruit, twice dead, plucked up by the roots;

Raging waves of the sea, foaming out their own shame; wandering stars, to whom is reserved the blackness of darkness for ever.

And Enoch also, the seventh from Adam, prophesied of these, saying, Behold, the Lord cometh with ten thousands of his saints,

To execute judgment upon all, and to convince all that are ungodly among them of all their ungodly deeds which they have ungodly committed, and of all their hard speeches which ungodly sinners have spoken against him.

These are murmurers, complainers, walking after their own lusts, and their mouth speaketh great swelling words, having men's persons in admiration because of advantage.

But, beloved, remember ye the words which were spoken before of the apostles of our Lord Jesus Christ;

How that they told you there should be mockers in the last time, who should walk after their own ungodly lusts.

These be they who separate themselves, sensual, having not the Spirit.

But ye, beloved, building up yourselves on your most holy faith, praying in the Holy Ghost,

Keep yourselves in the love of God, looking for the mercy of our Lord Jesus Christ unto eternal life.

And of some have compassion, making a difference:

And others save with fear, pulling them out of the fire; hating even the garment spotted by the flesh.

Now unto him that is able to keep you from falling, and to present you faultless before the presence of his glory with exceeding joy,

To the only wise God our Saviour, be glory and majesty, dominion and power, both now and ever. Amen (Jude 1:5-25).

Paul warned the Thessalonian Church not to be overzealous in either identifying the Antichrist at the end of time, setting dates for Christ's return, or looking for Him physically on the earth. He even warns us against thinking that He has already come and gone again. Why are we so eager to see the world end when there is so much work left for us to do in it? Never has God left Himself without a witness in this world, and we are that witness. Christ will come at the appointed time; meanwhile, the world seeps back into chaos without Him, as the Church has, once more, been cleverly neutralized and "taken out of the way." There is no a second chance for the lost. Read your Bible. There is no fly-by second coming 'rapture,' a second chance, and then a third return in judgment. This is an extremely dangerous man-made doctrine with misinterpretations that are unsubstantiated by the rest of Scripture. Do not follow the false prophets, which will multiply rapidly in these last days. How easy it is to take us "out of the way" when we are not thoroughly Bible and common sense based in our understanding of the ways of God.

And they shall say to you, See here; or, see there: go not after them, nor follow them.

For as the lightning, that lighteneth out of the one part under heaven, shineth unto the other part under heaven; so shall also the Son of man be in his day (Luke 17:23-24).

SECTION V

JOHN'S REVELATION

Return, O Lord, how long? and let it repent thee concerning thy servants.

O satisfy us early with thy mercy; that we may rejoice and be glad all our days. (Ps 90:13-14)

INTRODUCTION TO REVELATION

THINGS TO REMEMBER

I went to a Cirque du Soleil performance one Christmas with my youngest daughter and two grown granddaughters. In an odd sort of way, it reminded me of the book of Revelation. The actors, acrobats, singers and performers were above us, below us, in front of and behind us, and even flying in from every side. There was so much going on that it was impossible for me to see what was really going on. Finally, my granddaughters got me to focus on the action of the main plot and characters, where things became much simpler under their expert guidance and direction of where to look next. They had seen the production before and knew where the action was coming from and where it was going to; so now, they could enjoy all the performances without ever losing sight of the beautiful story that it told.

The book of Revelation is that vision which is provided for our journey home, literally. *It is understandable.* Please do not waste this precious gift on nonsense, speculation, false prophets and hate propaganda. It is not the intention of this section to introduce something new into the debate or even to line by line try to interpret it. The objective here is to keep you focused on what is really happening in the story and to offer you some very old insights into early church practices and beliefs that may not be familiar to you—but may increase your awareness of what John truly sees.

Foremost to remember in the vision is where John is located in it. God not only rules eternally from Eternity, but He rules from Eternity while continuously remaining present in every moment of time. God reigns supreme in ultimate and infinite power and authority—there is no other god but God alone. There is no past, no present and no future with God. There is not even a where of God as He rules time and creation from a constant and ever-present state of being and of knowing. Keep all of this in mind when you are reading Revelation and see if you can visualize the Creation's greater glory as we follow John through that open door and see what he saw from the vantage point of where he is seeing it:

> After this I looked, and, behold, a door was opened in heaven: and the first voice which I heard was as it were of a trumpet talking with me; which said, Come up hither, and I will shew thee things which must be hereafter.

> And immediately I was in the spirit: and, behold, a throne was set in heaven, and one sat on the throne (Rev 4:1-2).

At first reading, the overwhelming symbolism of John's vision blinds us to what is being revealed; however, in subsequent readings (and with the advice and insight of some very wise, very inspired, and very, very old friends), we see that the book itself is written within the characteristic apocalyptic style of the rest of the Bible. Apocalyptic style warns of impending doom and destruction on those who have refused God's authority but promises reward and blessing to those who welcome it—much as our Advent season brings both warning and promise. It is John's Revelation that finally fits all of the rest of the Bible's pieces together into that one particular story, that one single plot, into a picture that can only be observed from outside of time's ordered progression of events. This is where John is now standing as he gives us his vision.

Another thing to consider when reading this book is that Holy Scripture is not a composite of "hidden codes" (as some have claimed) any more than a good book of physics is about numerology. God is not only the writer but the underwriter, the guarantor, of all of the laws that He has fashioned to run the Creation—and anything that He reveals to us is certain to contain these three laws:

1. God's laws for the order and operation of the Creation;

2. God's structure, meaning and purpose for the Creation; and,

3. What He requires of what He has made.

If you have read the preceding chapters of this book first, you should already have those three keys well in hand and are ready to unlock John's vision. The following may seem difficult, but just keep reading and it will clarify itself. (Honestly, it will.)

St. Augustine explains:

> . . . it is for the same reason that philosophers have aimed at a threefold division of science, or rather, were enabled to see that there was a threefold division (for they did not invent, but only discovered it), of which one part is called physical, another logical, the third ethical. The Latin equivalents of these names are now naturalized in the writings of many authors, so that these divisions are called natural, rational, and moral.[1]

Now of these three sciences, only the natural laws can be physically measured, but the rational and the moral laws can be measured and demonstrated through their application to the physical—in other words, we can see them by and in what they do. This basic principal can also be applied to seeing God in the universe: We can see Him in what He does (in the natural) and know Him (in the rational) by what He requires of us (in the moral). If ever we can truly see the face of God in Scripture, we can see Him in the cohesive whole of the book of John's Revelation as demonstrated within this "threefold division of science."

The math, the how and the why of God creating, the progressive movement of time within the timelessness of Eternity, the natural moral law written within us and even our own ability to understand such things, all of this figures large in John's Revelation. But so that the explanation does not get more complicated than the book itself, just think of it like this:

It is a book which has but one story and one main hero, who has but one main love interest, and one really bad guy who keeps popping up and is out to spoil everything. The book is divided from beginning to end (Part 1 and Part 2) by seven main divisions and lots of action coming from three dynamic locations. (The three locations identify the energies and forces which give life to the vision's story, both within and outside of time.) *And yes, I know that I need to break that down further:*

1. Revelation's story is divided cleanly into two parts which are formed from a unified total of seven main divisions (Part 1 contains the first six divisions and Part 2 is formed from the seventh).

2. In addition, the entire book is animated by three constantly moving, dynamic mysteries—like a wheel spinning within a wheel spinning within a wheel—three mysteries. but all three revealing only one story.

3. These three mysteries are told through the threefold division of science: the physical, the logical and the ethical.

Still complicated, I know, but just keep reading.

You and I can both look at the stars and see that they travel, but you must explain to me how they travel and by what laws they must travel. In the case of the early church, she not only explains by what means they travel, but early Judeo-Christianity can also tell you the purpose and the meaning of their trip: the physical (natural), the logical (rational), and the ethical (God's good purpose for what He is creating). We can solve all three of these mysteries by standing where John stood and seeing what he saw in his vision.

Something else to remember while you are reading John's Revelation: All that is not God was and is made by Him and He called it good when He made it. The goodness of God, the goodness of the Creation that He made, the much-misunderstood term *predestination* in the question of good and evil and the mystery of the eternal now being always present in the flow of time—these statements also welcome you into the vision of the throne room of God.

Before we start our journey through Revelation though, it is important to clear up the differences between these two words: *predetermination* and *predestination*:

Predetermination: Not to create those whom you know will choose wrongly would be pre-determination. To create only those who would choose rightly would be pre-determination.

Predestination: To create creatures with the power to freely choose for themselves, the Creator having the foreknowledge of what they will freely choose, creates them anyway. That is predestination. We cannot choose God without the ability to not choose God.

Jesus chose Judas.

Judas chose thirty pieces of silver.

God saw this from the beginning, but He created Judas anyway.

Jesus chose him anyway.

Jesus died for him, anyway.

Jesus offered Himself to him, anyway.

One thing more: The modern difficultly in understanding John's Revelation today stems, in part, from Christians who are making a great profit by selling false doctrines to others—and many more have wasted their lives setting dates and times and trying to identify the antichrists. If we are constantly watching for the storms on the seas and searching for the dragons that swim in them, we will never get our little ship to port with its precious cargo. All of the events of mankind's history spring forth from Adam's personal creation and culminate in Jesus' second coming when He gathers together His faithful people unto Himself and pronounces final judgment on an idolatrous world. It is impossible to find a period of history when nation did not rise up against nation and lies and deceptions did not fill and rule the earth.

Christians have put countless souls in grave danger by adding to the book of Revelation doctrines that are simply not there.

We search the skies every morning to remind ourselves that He is coming back soon. But we search the skies as we are going out the door to work in His vineyard.

Next: Coming to the truth of John's vision may be as simple as understanding some Revelation's important numbers. Are you good at math? Well, God certainly is because He is not only the Creator of those numbers, but He is the Super Law which guides them while they work.

THE STRUCTURE OF THE CREATION

DIVISIONS AND MEANINGS

The book of John's Revelation consists of seven main divisions or visions or series of visions, which are themselves divided (roughly) into seven parts: 7 x 7 = 49. Forty-nine is the year of the Jewish completion of slavery and payment of debt in the Old Testament. The next year is the 50th year of the Jubilee, which is the Jewish year of atonement and freedom—again, type and antitype of what John sees taking place in Heaven as it is being played out here on earth.

And thou shalt number seven sabbaths of years unto thee, seven times seven years; and the space of the seven sabbaths of years shall be unto thee forty and nine years.

Then shalt thou cause the trumpet of the jubile to sound on the tenth day of the seventh month, in the day of atonement shall ye make the trumpet sound throughout all your land.

And ye shall hallow the fiftieth year, and proclaim liberty throughout all the land unto all the inhabitants thereof: it shall be a jubile unto you; and ye shall return every man unto his possession, and ye shall return every man unto his family (Lev 25:8-10).

(Even though you may not understand the divisions right away, you will. Be patient with the explanation of its structure and you will begin to see the beautiful story that it reveals. That's why it is called *Revelation.*)

The seven divisions of the main vision are preceded by the Introduction, Prologue and Blessing of St. John, and are followed by the Epilogue to the whole of the Holy Bible. These divisions are very loosely borrowed from the numbering of the chapter and verse divisions of Revelation which are found in J. D. Davis's *Davis Dictionary of the Bible.*[1] I have then taken the liberty of forming these divisions into two parts: the first six divisions form Part I and the seventh is the whole of Part II. Inserted are italicized explanations to give the whole a more comprehensible structure.

SUMMARY PART I: THE BATTLE FOR THE SOUL OF MANKIND

First Division:

Revelation 1:9-3:22. The vision of the Presence of the Glorified Christ standing within the Church (the seven lamp stands) holding the seven stars in His right hand, accompanied by His messages to each of the seven Churches and, through them, to us. His two-fold message is to repent and to persevere.

Second Division:

Revelation 4:1-8:5. The Vision of God, His Throne, the 24 elders and the four living creatures, and the worship of Heaven which reveals the liturgy of Heaven and of Earth. The Lamb of God as He opens the scroll and its seven seals. *Watch for the silence between the sixth and the seventh seals* as the prayers of God's people rise and fill the heavens with their sweet incense.

Here we must pause to explain the scroll. The scroll is the whole of Scripture which can only be revealed and understood through the sacrifice of the Christ of God, the worthy Lamb that was slain. But as the Lamb begins opening the understanding of Scripture to the faithful, the judgments for those who have forsaken God (judgments which are contained within that same scroll) begin to fall upon the unbelieving world in increasing severity.

The Bible itself has seven natural divisions: 1. the five books of the Law; 2. the books of History; 3. the books of Wisdom; 4. the books of Prophecy; 5. the Four Gospels; and, 6. the Acts and the Letters of the Apostles. 7. The Revelation of St. John is the seventh and final division and is the key to unlocking (unsealing) the mysteries of the other six.

Between the end of the opening of the sixth seal (the book of Jude) and the opening of the seventh seal (the book of Revelation), there is a dramatic pause as the faithful are sealed in their foreheads with the seal of the Living God before the throne of God's justice and judgment. Jude's letter is God's final offer of warning and of mercy to the sixth day—while Revelation demonstrates the glory of the Seventh Day of the Creation.

This is important: The Church Age is, and always has been, the Age of the Great Tribulation. In the sealing of the faithful, the faithful are protected from the Final Judgment and from the Second Death. We are not protected from the Great Tribulation, which purifies and purges us as it simultaneously calls out to an unrepentant world to repent before it is too late.

Third Division:

Revelation 8:6-9:19, Revelation 10 and 11. The judgment and the justice of God within the sounding of the trumpets which is poured out upon the unrepentant world. After the sixth trumpet and before the seventh trumpet are two extra visions: the undisclosed mystery contained in the little book which John ate in Revelation 10; and the mystery of the two witnesses in Revelation 11 (very likely the witnesses of the Law and the Prophets, their actions perfectly following the actions of Moses and Elijah: fire, drought, turning waters into blood, striking the earth with plagues).

The two olive trees are most probably the witnesses of the Old and New Testaments (but which may also refer back to Zacharia's story of the rebuilding of the nation of Israel after the Babylonian exile, a story which relates to the offices of king and of priest of a nation which is called out to be holy). Both of these are types of the Old Israel and the New Jerusalem. The Law and the Prophets form a single witness of the Old Covenant. The fulfillment of the Old Covenant is the witness of the New Covenant. Whether these two testimonies are embodied within two actual individuals at the end of time or whether the two witnesses of the two Covenants are incorporated within the total body of believers, we should be comforted in knowing that even their deaths will serve as a sign of Christ's imminent appearing, a sign which is given to the entire world.

The first pause was to seal God's martyrs (witnesses) on their foreheads and to pour forth their prayers before His throne. The second pause is to give them space and time to witness the world before the last trumpet sounds final judgment. The numbers one through six in Revelation are a warning of judgment. The number seven in Revelation is both final judgment for the lost and eternal rest for God's people.

Fourth Division:

Revelation 11:19 and Revelation 12, 13, and 14. The Vision of the Church in confrontation with the powers of evil through the Vision of the Woman, the Christ Child, the Dragon and his minions.

And the temple of God was opened in heaven, and there was seen in his temple the ark of his testament: and there were lightnings, and voices, and thunderings, and an earthquake, and great hail (Rev 11:19).

And there appeared a great wonder in heaven; a woman clothed with the sun, and the moon under her feet, and upon her head a crown of twelve stars:

And she being with child cried, travailing in birth, and pained to be delivered.

And there appeared another wonder in heaven; and behold a great red dragon, having seven heads and ten horns, and seven crowns upon his heads.

And his tail drew the third part of the stars of heaven, and did cast them to the earth: and the dragon stood before the woman which was ready to be delivered, for to devour her child as soon as it was born.

And she brought forth a man child, who was to rule all nations with a rod of iron: and her child was caught up unto God, and to his throne.

And the woman fled into the wilderness, where she hath a place prepared of God, that they should feed her there a thousand two hundred and threescore days (Rev 12:1-6).

And the dragon was wroth with the woman, and went to make war with the remnant of her seed, which keep the commandments of God, and have the testimony of Jesus Christ (Rev 12:17).

Of special note to some Protestant Churches is the often-overlooked verse of Revelation 11:19. While we are busy looking for the Ark of the Old Covenant (Testament) on earth, here an Ark is revealed that is already in Heaven in the very next verse, Revelation 12: 1.

Mary was given to the Church at the foot of the Cross when Jesus gave His mother to John: "Woman, behold thy son!" "Behold thy mother!" (John 19:26, 27), at which time the Church then becomes her children who are relentlessly pursued by the Dragon. Both actual and spiritual, the Ark of the Covenant of the Old Testament is the type of its antitype, Mary. Mary has always been a symbol of the Motherhood of the Church and of its children to which it gives birth, and she does so again in the vision of John, right here, where she is clothed in the light of the sun and adorned with the garland of the twelve stars of the Apostles. The moon under her feet has no light of its own but is set in the heavens to be a reflection of the light of the sun, which is also a picture of the Church reflecting the light of the Christ of God upon a dark world. Mary is also a symbol of Israel giving birth to their Messiah and of the Church bringing forth the fruit of its children. As she flees into the wilderness, the Dragon sends a flood after her, the earth opens its mouth and swallows up the flood—type and antitype of Israel trapped at the Red Sea. The Dragon pursues her other children, and, as we have seen both in the past and in the present, both Church and Synagogue have suffered intense persecution throughout their collective histories.

Now watch this: Each Christian should mirror the light of Christ on earth as the moon mirrors the sun and as we follow in His footsteps and carry on His work. The whole of the Church together on earth is a type of Mary as we also labor in birth pains to bring forth the Children of God. There is a wealth of Early Christian symbolism going on in these simple verses. Please do not overlook it!

The direct opposite of Jesus, the Christ of God, is the Antichrist. The direct opposite of the Church, of the New Jerusalem, of Mary as the Ark of the New Covenant—is the filthy, drunken Whore that rides upon the Beast of Babylon, that dreadful city that leads her children into perdition and into the eternal damnation of its own hell.

Fifth Division:

Revelation 15 and 16 contain the seven bowls of the Seven Last Judgments poured out because mankind does not repent; rather, it curses God and thus brings damnation down upon itself. Note: The vision opens with the praise of the Saints.

> And they sing the song of Moses the servant of God, and the song of the Lamb, saying, Great and marvellous are thy

works, Lord God Almighty; just and true are thy ways, thou King of saints.

Who shall not fear thee, O Lord, and glorify thy name? for thou only art holy: for all nations shall come and worship before thee; for thy judgments are made manifest (Rev 15:3-4).

Sixth Division:

Revelation 18, 19 and 20. Final Judgment, which culminates in the Great White Throne Judgment: The Victory of the Christ over the harlot city of Babylon, which is Satan's deformed and pathetic imitation of the New Jerusalem, the City of God. The pause between the sixth and the seventh visions assures us once again that the Bride of Christ is always victorious in Christ, even in and through her tribulation period here on earth. The Bridegroom is always there to shelter His bride from that dreadful Final Judgment.

PART II: BEHOLDING THE FACE OF GOD

Seventh Division:

Revelation 21. The Marriage of the Bride of Christ as she rests in glory with her Divine Bridegroom in the New Jerusalem, in the full realization of the meaning of our creation. What we have seen in a glass darkly, we now see Face to face in the clear light of the Eighth Day, the first day of the New Creation.

Part I of Revelation culminates in the six divisions of the Creation, followed by the Final Judgment and the separation of God's people from it.

Part II begins in the New Jerusalem at the everlasting Wedding Feast of the Lamb. It is eternal, timeless and infinite. It is never-ending.

Now, it is time to tackle some of Revelation's important numbers and to perhaps better understand what they are really describing to us.

THE NUMBERS OF HEAVEN

THE DOMINION OF CHRIST

Just as it has greatly enlarged our perspective of God, Revelation now opens wide the door to God's Kingdom. For example, if we want to know about the Millennial Reign of the Christ (which so preoccupies the modern-day mind), we can begin by asking and answering a few simple questions.

Q. Where in the Bible does it say Millennium?

A. It doesn't. It says 1,000.

Q. Well then, does the Church have a different understanding of the number 1,000 than the exact number 1,000?

A. Yes, it does, because the 1,000-year reign of Christ can no more be understood as a calendar count of 365-day years than can a 24-hour solar earth day be understood as the first day of the Creation. Nor can the one-hour reign of the kings in Revelation 17 mean one 60-minute hour of time for the ten kings and their kingdoms:

> And the ten horns which thou sawest are ten kings, which have received no kingdom as yet; but receive power as kings one hour with the beast (Rev 17:12).

Q. So what does the 1,000-year reign of Christ designate then?

A. It designates the reign of Christ within His Church. The Great Tribulation period is now—it is the Age of the Church and we are living in it. In John's vision, more than in any other book of the Bible, we see how God's eternal calculations exceed and overwhelm the simple physics of His Creation. We must have a clear definition or an explanation of the number 1,000 before we can start making doctrine out of it, so here it is:

The number 1,000 is the ecclesiastical number which signifies incalculable immensity, perfection, completion and wholeness—the dimensions of which are known to God alone.

The 1,000-year period of Satan being chained in the abyss is the indeterminate time between Christ's complete victory over Satan at His resurrection and Christ's Second Coming in the Final Judgment. The Age of the Church, in time, is an indeterminate number which only God knows; and in which (although God allows severe persecution and difficulties for her in it) we still flourish and grow and fill the earth. In fact, the Church always grows fastest, deepest, longest, tallest, strongest, purest and most perfectly in times of trouble and purging. The peaceable kingdom of Christ is embodied within His Church, in the Age of the Church here on earth.

Again, the number 1,000 is the ecclesiastical number which signifies incalculable immensity, perfection, completion and wholeness. With this definition firmly in mind, we can revisit some of Revelation's references to this number.

> And I beheld, and I heard the voice of many angels round about the throne and the beasts and the elders: and the number of them was ten thousand times ten thousand, and thousands of thousands;

> Saying with a loud voice, Worthy is the Lamb that was slain to receive power, and riches, and wisdom, and strength, and honour, and glory, and blessing (Rev 5:11-12).

> 11:3 And I will give power unto my two witnesses, and they shall prophesy a thousand two hundred and threescore days, clothed in sackcloth. (Link with 12:6 below)

> 11:13 And the same hour was there a great earthquake, and the tenth part of the city fell, and in the earthquake were slain of men seven thousand: and the remnant were affrighted, and gave glory to the God of heaven.

> 12:6 And the woman fled into the wilderness, where she hath a place prepared of God, that they should feed her there a thousand two hundred and threescore days.

14:1 And I looked, and, lo, a Lamb stood on the mount Sion, and with him an hundred forty and four thousand, having his Father's name written in their foreheads.

14:3 And they sung as it were a new song before the throne, and before the four beasts, and the elders: and no man could learn that song but the hundred and forty and four thousand, which were redeemed from the earth.

14:20 And the winepress was trodden without the city, and blood came out of the winepress, even unto the horse bridles, by the space of a thousand and six hundred furlongs.

20:2 And he laid hold on the dragon, that old serpent, which is the Devil, and Satan, and bound him a thousand years

20:3 And cast him into the bottomless pit, and shut him up, and set a seal upon him, that he should deceive the nations no more, till the thousand years should be fulfilled: and after that he must be loosed a little season.

20:4 And I saw thrones, and they sat upon them, and judgment was given unto them: and I saw the souls of them that were beheaded for the witness of Jesus, and for the word of God, and which had not worshipped the beast, neither his image, neither had received his mark upon their foreheads, or in their hands; and they lived and reigned with Christ a thousand years.

20:5 But the rest of the dead lived not again until the thousand years were finished. This is the first resurrection.

20:7 And when the thousand years are expired, Satan shall be loosed out of his prison.

Peter comforts us, the Church, through our long, dark nights of waiting for Christ's return:

> But the heavens and the earth, which are now, by the same word are kept in store, reserved unto fire against the day of judgment and perdition of ungodly men.
>
> But, beloved, be not ignorant of this one thing, that one day is with the Lord as a thousand years, and a thousand years as one day.
>
> The Lord is not slack concerning his promise, as some men count slackness; but is longsuffering to us-ward, not willing that any should perish, but that all should come to repentance (2 Peter 3:7-9).

Understanding that God's Eternity does not march to earth's clocks and calendars is as crucial to understanding Scripture as is our understanding that God's infinity and eternity will not fit into that neat little box that we have prepared for them. Our little box is tiny indeed compared to God's Infinite Cube of the New Jerusalem which just got a whole lot bigger. If the number 1,000 is the ecclesiastical number which signifies immensity—a huge and indeterminate number that can only be known by God Himself—

then this definition is fundamental also in describing the measurements of the City of the New Jerusalem, the New Holy of Holies, *cubed.*

Question: So, is the New Jerusalem really only as large as the United States, cubed, which are the measurements allotted to it in Revelation?

Answer: Now that we understand that the number 1,000 incorporates God's dimensions, not ours, we can link the number twelve to it and see what we get for the size of the New Jerusalem, the City of God.

Twelve is the number of foundation, of worship and of government. It stands for the twelve tribes of Israel, for the twelve Apostles of Christ and for the twelve angels that guard our gates. Twelve times twelve is the foundational number of Judeo-Christianity, 144, times our heavenly hosts, the angels who guard our gates—all multiplied by 1,000, by immensity.

Therefore, our city's length, breadth, and height are equal, making it a perfect cube: 12,000 x 12,000 x 12,000 = the City of God.

> And the city lieth foursquare, and the length is as large as the breadth: and he measured the city with the reed, twelve thousand furlongs. The length and the breadth and the height of it are equal (Rev 21:16).

The cubic measurements of the city are thus: The Old Covenant Foundation x the New Covenant Foundation x the Angelic Foundation, indicating the perfection and totality of the Creation in worship of its Creator. Within the City of God, within the Holy of Holies, the City of the New Jerusalem resides: 12 x 12 x 12 x immensity (indicated by 1,000) = a cube of such vast design that only God can know its true size. If you are looking for an exact number here, you won't find it. How can you calculate immensity, eternity, and infinity? And then, how would you multiply that by the three foundations it rests upon?

Question: And we'll be there someday, by and by?

Answer: We are already members there in our present capacity as the Church Militant, the Church that is still in time, fighting for the soul of Adam. This is one of the most important things that John's vision tells us. The Church Triumphant is made up of those who have gone on before us but who are still actively worshipping and interceding with us before the throne of God. No matter on what level of existence the Church is found, it will always be the one true Body of Christ, His Bride. Whether in the heavens or here on earth, we are One in Him. The twelve tribes of Israel, the olive tree into which we were grafted, are called out by name, 12 x 12 x 1000 in the Book of Revelation, as well as the thousands of the faithful that follow them:

> After this I beheld, and, lo, a great multitude, which no man could number, of all nations, and kindreds, and people, and

> tongues, stood before the throne, and before the Lamb,
> clothed with white robes, and palms in their hands;
>
> And cried with a loud voice, saying, Salvation to our God
> which sitteth upon the throne, and unto the Lamb (Rev 7:9-
> 10).

Here is the redeemed of all mankind (angels not included this time). The 144,000 (12 x 12 x 1000) are like the voice of many waters, and like the voice of loud thunder, as we sing the song that only the redeemed can understand. If you don't receive anything else from this chapter, at least take this away with you.

> And I looked, and, lo, a Lamb stood on the mount Sion, and
> with him an hundred forty and four thousand, having his
> Father's name written in their foreheads.
>
> And I heard a voice from heaven, as the voice of many
> waters, and as the voice of a great thunder: and I heard the
> voice of harpers harping with their harps:
>
> And they sung as it were a new song before the throne, and
> before the four beasts, and the elders: and no man could
> learn that song but the hundred and forty and four thousand,
> which were redeemed from the earth (Rev 14:1-3).

This song is the song of thanksgiving for our redemption. It is a song that only the redeemed have learned and only the redeemed of mankind can sing it: "and no man could learn that song but the hundred and forty and four thousand, which were redeemed from the earth."

Why are the redeemed called virgins? Because we cannot now be accused of spiritual or adulterous defilement against our Lord. We have been redeemed—bought back—by His love and His sacrifice. Renewed. Born again. Washed clean in His blood. His Bride is a virgin bride.

> Come now, and let us reason together, saith the Lord: though your sins be as scarlet, they shall be as white as snow; though they be red like crimson, they shall be as wool (Is 1:18).

These are the numbers of Heaven as they are found in Revelation. Next are the numbers of mankind and of earth as they are revealed to us through John's vision.

THE NUMBERS OF MANKIND

THE SEVEN DAYS OF THE CREATION

As we have demonstrated the numbers of Heaven, we can now turn our attention to Revelation's numbers which are indicative of mankind within the Seven Days of the Creation.

The first of these numbers is the number four and the multiples of the number four which stand for the whole of the Creation—but in particular, for the world of mankind (male and female) in relation to its Creator.

And when he had taken the book, the four beasts and four and twenty elders fell down before the Lamb, having every one of them harps, and golden vials full of odours, which are the prayers of saints (Rev 5:8).

The twenty-four elders of Revelation hold harps of praise, and as they release the prayers of the saints from the golden bowls that they hold, a very earthly picture is produced of the unity of the

Church in Heaven with the Church on Earth as we join together with them in praising the Lamb of our Sacrifice:

> And they sung a new song, saying, Thou art worthy to take the book, and to open the seals thereof: for thou wast slain, and hast redeemed us to God by thy blood out of every kindred, and tongue, and people, and nation;

> And hast made us unto our God kings and priests: and we shall reign on the earth (Rev 5:9-10).

Why is it that no one seems to see the last of that last verse? ". . . and we shall reign on the earth?" Where did we get the idea that our souls are like helium balloons that are released to just float around the heavens after death? We don't become angels or even like the angels. We were created from the earth, earthly, quickened by the breath of God: and we shall be raised in the likeness of our resurrected Lord. God loves the earth and all that He created to be in it. New heavens. New us. New earth and all that God gave mankind dominion over in the beginning.

> Nevertheless we, according to his promise, look for new heavens and a new earth, wherein dwelleth righteousness (2 Peter 3:13).

> And I saw a new heaven and a new earth: for the first heaven and the first earth were passed away; and there was no more sea.

And I John saw the holy city, new Jerusalem, coming down from God out of heaven, prepared as a bride adorned for her husband (Rev 21: 1-2).

Jesus was resurrected in His physical, albeit glorified, body. He could be touched. He walked through closed doors. He retained the marks of his crucifixion. He ate. He appeared, He disappeared, He ascended into Heaven—and in like manner, as He disappeared, He will return to be with us forever. Will there be animals on our new earth? Did not God create the heavens and the earth and all that was in them? And did He not declare them good? Nothing of that good will forever be lost to us. It was created for God's pleasure and gifted to us from the beginning.

And after eight days again his disciples were within, and Thomas with them: then came Jesus, the doors being shut, and stood in the midst, and said, Peace be unto you.

Then saith he to Thomas, Reach hither thy finger, and behold my hands; and reach hither thy hand, and thrust it into my side: and be not faithless, but believing.

And Thomas answered and said unto him, My Lord and my God (John 20:26-28).

There are four corners which surround the Revelation: 1. Christ in Glory; 2. Christ in Tribulation through His Church Militant on earth; 3. Christ Triumphant over evil, rebellion and death; and, 4. Christ Reigning with His Bride in the New Jerusalem as past, present and future events stream together in the final climax of history.

> And before the throne there was a sea of glass like unto crystal: and in the midst of the throne, and round about the throne, were four beasts full of eyes before and behind.

> And the first beast was like a lion, and the second beast like a calf, and the third beast had a face as a man, and the fourth beast was like a flying eagle (Rev 4:6-7).

Around the throne in the Heaven of Revelation are four living creatures full of eyes in front and in back (the eyes indicating vigilance, wisdom and knowledge). These four creatures ("beasts," meaning created from the earth as opposed to the angels) are very important and instrumental to what is happening here on earth. In the early churches and in those churches that have kept their history, these same figures have been used to represent the four Evangelists. On the cover of many Bibles and in Christian art, the Alpha and the Omega symbols bookend the central image of the figure of the Christ of God. He stands with an open Bible in His left hand, his right hand is raised in blessing with two fingers held together and aloft, and the last three (two fingers and one thumb) forming a tight circle. The two fingers aloft declare the Christ of God as both fully human and fully divine and the single circle of three is indicative of the Trinitarian God Whom we worship. The Christ of God and the symbols of the four evangelists are depicted on the cover of Bibles because they open the door of our understanding to the whole of Scripture.

(A notable exception to this interpretation: "the four living creatures, each of them with six wings, are full of eyes all round" (Rev. 4:8) are thought by many to also personify the whole of the Creation itself in praise of its Creator. Christian tradition depicts them as the four Evangelists and thus unites the Worship and the Liturgy of the Creation with that of the worship and liturgy of the Church.)

Four angels stand at the four corners of the earth, holding the four winds of the earth, and to them, it was granted to harm the earth and the sea. There are four horns of the Golden Altar of earth's redemption and there are four angels which are bound at the River Euphrates.

Four is also the number of the history of the earth which culminates in the Beatific Vision of the Risen Savior: 1. The Fall of Adam; 2. God's Covenant Promise of a Messiah to Adam; 3. The Redemption of Adam, and; 4. The Final Judgment of Mankind.

The Four Horsemen of the Apocalypse ride from Heaven to earth as the seals of our understanding are opened.

Six is the number which has no rest in it because it is the number of incompletion and imperfection, of lack and of wanting: The number six is a finite number—it is limited. Its days are fixed, it has no bridge, and its end is already determined. Its identifying mark is turmoil as evidenced by the events of the Sixth Day portrayed in Revelation and within the Trinity of Perdition: 666. There is a noticeable and intensifying abyss between the numbers six and seven as we come closer to the cliff's edge of the Sixth Day in John's Revelation—and as the world of the Sixth Day finally falls over the cliff of Final Judgment, the Virgin Bride of Christ crosses her Bridge of Rest in Jesus which is the Seventh Day. As we come evermore closer to that cliff's edge in the progression of the chapters of Revelation, again and again, it signals that something is ending and that something even bigger is about to happen.

Seven is the number of completion and perfection and of rest from the day's work. Seven is the end of the matter: "It is finished." Seven is the number of totality, the entirety of a thing. Its importance in Scripture begs us to take another look at this recurring and inexhaustible number, the most mentioned number in the book of Revelation. Think of its meaning when you read these verses concerning "the seven Spirits of God."

Revelation:

> 1:4 John to the seven churches which are in Asia: Grace be unto you, and peace, from him which is, and which was, and which is to come; and from the seven Spirits which are before his throne;

3:1 And unto the angel of the church in Sardis write; These things saith he that hath the seven Spirits of God, and the seven stars; I know thy works, that thou hast a name that thou livest, and art dead.

4:5 And out of the throne proceeded lightnings and thunderings and voices: and there were seven lamps of fire burning before the throne, which are the seven Spirits of God.

5:6 And I beheld, and, lo, in the midst of the throne and of the four beasts, and in the midst of the elders, stood a Lamb as it had been slain, having seven horns and seven eyes, which are the seven Spirits of God sent forth into all the earth.

St John's gospel records:

In the last day, that great day of the feast, Jesus stood and cried, saying, If any man thirst, let him come unto me, and drink.

He that believeth on me, as the Scripture hath said, out of his belly shall flow rivers of living water.

(But this spake he of the Spirit, which they that believe on him should receive: for the Holy Ghost was not yet given; because that Jesus was not yet glorified) (John 7:37-39).

What do the church fathers say about these seven Spirits? The Jews speak of seven Archangels who stand before God's throne

(and those may be the Seven Stars also), but many of the fathers of
our early Christian faith thought otherwise of the seven Spirits. St.
Ambrose, the Bishop of Milan, wrote in the late 4th century about
the Holy Spirit of God as that great, flowing River of Revelation in
his exposition, "On the Holy Spirit," Book I:

> . . . This is the great River which flows always and never
> fails. And not only a river, but also one of copious stream
> and overflowing greatness, as also David said: "The stream
> of the river makes glad the city of God."

For neither is that city, the heavenly Jerusalem, watered by
the channel of any earthly river, but that Holy Spirit,
proceeding from the Fount of Life, by a short draught of
Whom we are satiated, seems to flow more abundantly
among those celestial Thrones, Dominions and Powers,
Angels and Archangels, rushing in the full course of the
seven virtues of the Spirit. For if a river rising above its
banks overflows, how much more does the Spirit, rising
above every creature, when He touches as it were low-lying
fields of our minds, make glad that heavenly nature of the
creatures with the larger fertility of His sanctification.

And let it not trouble you that either here it is said "rivers,"
John vii. 38. or elsewhere "seven Spirits," Rev. v. 6. for by
the sanctification of these seven gifts of the Spirit, as Isaiah
said, Isa. xi. 2. is signified the fullness of all virtue; the
Spirit of wisdom and understanding, the Spirit of counsel

and strength, the Spirit of knowledge and godliness, and the Spirit of the fear of God. One, then, is the River, but many the channels of the gifts of the Spirit. This River, then, goes forth from the Fount of Life.[1]

So then, let us ask God to grant us also the fullness of His Holy Spirit and with Him, His sevenfold abundance of virtue that we may understand correctly what He desires that we should know.

There are seven final Beatitudes of Scripture which are promised in John's Revelation:

1:3 Blessed is he that readeth, and they that hear the words of this prophecy, and keep those things which are written therein: for the time is at hand.

14:13 And I heard a voice from heaven saying unto me, Write, Blessed are the dead which die in the Lord from henceforth: Yea, saith the Spirit, that they may rest from their labours; and their works do follow them.

16:15 Behold, I come as a thief. Blessed is he that watcheth, and keepeth his garments, lest he walk naked, and they see his shame.

19:9 And he saith unto me, Write, Blessed are they which are called unto the marriage supper of the Lamb. And he saith unto me, These are the true sayings of God.

20:6 Blessed and holy is he that hath part in the first resurrection: on such the second death hath no power, but they shall be priests of God and of Christ, and shall reign with him a thousand years.

22:7 Behold, I come quickly: blessed is he that keepeth the sayings of the prophecy of this book.

22:14 Blessed are they that do his commandments, that they may have right to the tree of life, and may enter in through the gates into the city.

The Church is represented in Revelation by the Seven Churches to whom the messages are given, indicating the Church of all time. The seventh angel announces the end of the tribulation.

And the seventh angel poured out his vial into the air; and there came a great voice out of the temple of heaven, from the throne, saying, It is done (Rev 16:17).

The 1,260 days or 42 months or 3½ years are all halves of the number seven. God's two witnesses will witness and suffer for a half time. The book is sweet in our mouth but sour in our persecutions.

But the court which is without the temple leave out, and measure it not; for it is given unto the Gentiles: and the holy city shall they tread under foot forty and two months.

And I will give power unto my two witnesses, and they shall prophesy a thousand two hundred and threescore days, clothed in sackcloth (Rev 11:2-3).

Exactly halfway through the completion number of 7 is 3½, both preceding and following it. It usually refers to a time of witnessing and of great persecution and suffering: God's Old Covenant with Israel; God's New Covenant with Christians. In the case of the book of Revelation and until the final trumpet sounds and the final bowl is poured out, that is what the Church has been doing ever since the Ascension of Christ and the outpouring of the Holy Spirit on Pentecost. The Great War was won at the Crucifixion and the Resurrection, but Revelation's Chapters 12, 13 and 14 seem to hand over battles to us that must now be fought and won by the Church—the whole of which is the Body of Christ here on earth supported by the prayers of the Body of Christ in Heaven. Revelation assures us that we can overcome evil by the Blood of the Lamb and by our testimony. It also teaches us that time itself ends with the Last Judgment.

Now then, consider that it would be impossible to win a battle, or to fight a battle if you and I have gone missing and are not even in the battle! And the weapon that we must carry into that battle is the most powerful weapon of all: the Word of God.

> For the word of God is quick, and powerful, and sharper than any two-edged sword, piercing even to the dividing asunder of soul and spirit, and of the joints and marrow, and is a discerner of the thoughts and intents of the heart.

Neither is there any creature that is not manifest in his sight: but all things are naked and opened unto the eyes of him with whom we have to do.

Seeing then that we have a great high priest, that is passed into the heavens, Jesus the Son of God, let us hold fast our profession (Heb 4:12-14).

Now that we have a basic understanding of Revelation's most important numbers and themes, we can finally look at the three constantly moving, dynamic mysteries that propel the vision—the wheel within the wheel within the wheel—three interlocking mysteries that tell but one story:

1. Revelation as the Bride of Heaven and Earth.

2. Revelation as the Liturgy of Heaven and Earth.

3. Revelation's Two Cities.

SECTION VI

THE EIGHTH DAY

Make us glad according to the days wherein thou hast afflicted us, and the years wherein we have seen evil. Let thy work appear unto thy servants, and thy glory unto their children (Ps 90:15-16).

16

THE BRIDE OF THE NEW CREATION

THE EIGHTH DAY

Scientists are just now discovering what readers of the Bible have always known: There is space between the atoms of creation. And not only space but massive space.

God gave Jacob the vision of the heavenly ladder to tell Israel that there is space between the atoms of creation. God gave the Church a world-shaking Pentecost to demonstrate that there is space between the atoms of creation. Jesus physically appeared through closed and locked doors to assure us that there is something beyond the natural going on within nature. And John was given the Revelation not only to comfort and to strengthen us but also to open our eyes to the fact that the Church and the world itself are both transparent and permeable. There is Eternal space between the atoms of the Creation, and inside and outside of that space is the Eternal Energy and Essence of the Creator's absolute authority over all that He has created.

In the physical world of time and matter, of mass that occupies place, we see that God has left room for the timelessness of Eternity, not just to come and go and not just to statically exist, but space enough for Eternity to interact powerfully and constantly with and within time. In fact, without that space, without that interaction, any existence at all would be impossible.

Moses, Elijah and the Christ of God tell us in the Transfiguration that there is an inexplicable space into which Jesus calls us to follow Him up and out of the darkness of unknowing and into the brilliant light of knowing. And it is in the last book of the entire Bible where, more than in any other book, the heart of the Bible beats. It is the sum total. It is both the base camp of our climb and the summit of the mountain that we scale.

Through the humanity of Jesus, He is able to die; but through His Divinity, the Christ of God is able take up that life again as one whole and resurrected Eternal Being. It is through this miracle that Jesus establishes His Church and calls it forth from the world and into a place which is simply named the New Jerusalem, the City of God—the place of our Wedding Feast with the Sacrificial Lamb of God. And it is here also that space is truly folded in order that Heaven and earth can come together in the worship of their Creator: 12 x 12 x 12 x Immensity, Eternity, and Infinity—both within and outside of time. The Old Covenant, the New Covenant, and all the Angelic Hosts in union with one another and in active worship of our God as we present ourselves to Him. Here is the New Jerusalem—"Thy kingdom come, Thy will be done in earth, as it is in heaven" (Matt 6: 10). Here is the Church "in earth, as it is in heaven." It is here that our corporate worship is fulfilled within Christ's promise: "For where two or three are gathered together in my name, there am I in the midst of them" (Matt 18:20).

> If I have told you earthly things, and ye believe not, how shall ye believe, if I tell you of heavenly things? (John 3:12).

Consider these three Biblical revelations found in John's vision:

1. The Church not only has Christ living within it, but through its transparency and permeability, the Holy Spirit is able to create in us the witness of a living Christ to the world: "be it unto me according to thy word" we say with Mary as we accept our Savior into our own lives.

2. The Church has always been foreshadowed and overshadowed from Eternity by the New Jerusalem of Heaven, and through the vision of John's Revelation, we can also see how our own worship on earth is but a mirror of the worship of Heaven.

3. As the Old Covenant tent and temple worship of Israel within the Holy of Holies and upon its altar of sacrifice,

foreshadowed the Sacrifice of Christ in the New Covenant. In Revelation, we see the liturgy of the New Jerusalem duplicated in the Christian liturgy (public worship) of the Church here on earth.

If your church has taken you farther and farther away from the culture of the Judeo-Christianity of the very first church, you are less likely to see and understand John's vision. As Paul explains:

> Now of the things which we have spoken this is the sum: We have such an high priest, who is set on the right hand of the throne of the Majesty in the heavens;
>
> A minister of the sanctuary, and of the true tabernacle, which the Lord pitched, and not man.
>
> For every high priest is ordained to offer gifts and sacrifices: wherefore it is of necessity that this man have somewhat also to offer.
>
> For if he were on earth, he should not be a priest, seeing that there are priests that offer gifts according to the law:
>
> Who serve unto the example and shadow of heavenly things, as Moses was admonished of God when he was about to make the tabernacle: for, See, saith he, that thou make all things according to the pattern shewed to thee in the mount.
>
> But now hath he obtained a more excellent ministry, by how much also he is the mediator of a better covenant, which was established upon better promises (Heb 8:1-6).

The First Covenant Sanctuary had instructions on how its worship was to be conducted:

> According to all that I shew thee, after the pattern of the tabernacle, and the pattern of all the instruments thereof, even so shall ye make it (Ex 25:9).

Can we also see the liturgy of the New Covenant Sanctuary on earth within the liturgy of the worship of Heaven and revealed by John's vision?

The doorway to our faith is Justification. But now the time has come that we should not just enter through that doorway but allow ourselves to be lifted up into the New Jerusalem. Here it is that Jesus is taken up into the Transfiguration. Here it is that Aaron's rod that budded becomes the wood of the Crucifixion and the golden bowl of manna becomes the Marriage Feast of the Lamb for His Bride. The tablet of the Law is read and is satisfied, and we are justified. But it is here also, upon the Altar of Sacrifice, that the Christ of God pours out His blood for our salvation, in the New Jerusalem, on earth as it is in Heaven.

From the wounded side of Adam was born his bride, Eve, the mother of all living. From the tortured flesh and from the water and the blood that poured forth from the wounded side of Jesus, His Eternal Bride, the Church was born. "This is My Body." "This is My Blood." This is our Eucharistic Celebration. This is our Holy Communion. This is the Wedding Feast of the Lamb. This is the Heavenly Liturgy that should be reflected in our worship here on earth. Can we prove that what John saw in his vision is the pattern for the New Covenant liturgy?

The New Testament:

> It was therefore necessary that the patterns of things in the heavens should be purified with these; but the heavenly things themselves with better sacrifices than these.

> For Christ is not entered into the holy places made with hands, which are the figures of the true; but into heaven itself, now to appear in the presence of God for us:

> Nor yet that he should offer himself often, as the high priest entereth into the holy place every year with blood of others;

> For then must he often have suffered since the foundation of the world: but now once in the end of the world hath he appeared to put away sin by the sacrifice of himself.

> And as it is appointed unto men once to die, but after this the judgment:

> So Christ was once offered to bear the sins of many; and unto them that look for him shall he appear the second time without sin unto salvation (Heb 9:23-28).

So far, we should be somewhat on the same page, no matter your denomination. If not, then think about this: When we worship together, not only is Christ's Presence with us and in us all, but through Him also, we are present within the worship of Heaven itself. The Body of Christ is One Bride eternally, whether in Heaven or here on earth.

Again, can we see the liturgy of worship before the very throne of God in John's vision? The real question is, "How can we not see it!" And seeing it, how can we not "make everything according to the pattern which was shown you on the mountain"? The New Jerusalem is next.

17

THE LITURGY OF HEAVEN AND EARTH

THE NEW JERUSALEM

The culmination of liturgical worship is the Marriage Feast of the Lamb, "This is My Body." "This is My Blood." The Eucharist, the sacrament of Holy Communion, the Lord's Supper is the summit of our worship of God which is taken up into and united with the worship of Heaven—and multiplied throughout all of time and eternity like the loaves and the fishes which fed the 5,000.

And they sat down in ranks, by hundreds, and by fifties.

And when he had taken the five loaves and the two fishes, he looked up to heaven, and blessed, and brake the loaves, and gave them to his disciples to set before them; and the two fishes divided he among them all.

And they did all eat, and were filled.

And they took up twelve baskets full of the fragments, and of the fishes.

And they that did eat of the loaves were about five thousand men (Mark 6:40-44).

No matter how extravagant its imagery, the book of Revelation is a simple love story. It is all about the Groom's sacrificial love for His Bride and the Bride's rapt adoration of her Groom. It is a book of courtship from beginning to end, a courtship consummated with these words: "This is My Body." "This is My Blood." This is the Wedding Feast of the Lamb.

And as they were eating, Jesus took bread, and blessed it, and brake it, and gave it to the disciples, and said, Take, eat; this is my body.

And he took the cup, and gave thanks, and gave it to them, saying, Drink ye all of it;

For this is my blood of the new testament, which is shed for many for the remission of sins (Matt 26:26-28).

For where two or three are gathered together in my name, there am I in the midst of them (Matt 18:20).

PART I: THE LITURGY OF OUR WORSHIP

Revelation begins with John in worship: "I was in the Spirit on the Lord's day . . ." Jesus is always present within His Church and

His Church lives forever in Him in a gathering of time into Eternity, every time we come together to worship in His Name: "For where two or three are gathered together in my name, there am I in the midst of them (Matt 18:20).

> And I turned to see the voice that spake with me. And being turned, I saw seven golden candlesticks;
>
> And in the midst of the seven candlesticks one like unto the Son of man, clothed with a garment down to the foot, and girt about the paps with a golden girdle (Rev 1:12-13).
>
> The mystery of the seven stars which thou sawest in my right hand, and the seven golden candlesticks. The seven stars are the angels of the seven churches: and the seven candlesticks which thou sawest are the seven churches. (Rev 1:20).

The first thing that we notice about the liturgy of Revelation is Christ's call to repentance and to confession: "in my thoughts and in my words," declares the ancient prayer of confession, "in what I have done and in what I have failed to do." Our worship begins with a searching of our souls, with confession, forgiveness, and cleansing of whatever separates us from our Lord.

> Remember therefore from whence thou art fallen, and repent, and do the first works; or else I will come unto thee quickly, and will remove thy candlestick out of his place, except thou repent (Rev 2:5).

As many as I love, I rebuke and chasten: be zealous therefore, and repent (Rev 3:19).

"After these things," an open door appears in heaven. Not before. And as that door opens to you also, you have the opportunity to "come up hither" with John and see the things that he saw. But be careful, for here you are standing on Holy Ground.

Behold, I stand at the door, and knock: if any man hear my voice, and open the door, I will come in to him, and will sup with him, and he with me (Rev 3:20).

After this I looked, and, behold, a door was opened in heaven: and the first voice which I heard was as it were of a trumpet talking with me; which said, Come up hither, and I will shew thee things which must be hereafter.

And immediately I was in the spirit: and, behold, a throne was set in heaven, and one sat on the throne.

And he that sat was to look upon like a jasper and a sardine stone: and there was a rainbow round about the throne, in sight like unto an emerald.

And round about the throne were four and twenty seats: and upon the seats I saw four and twenty elders sitting, clothed in white raiment; and they had on their heads crowns of gold.

And out of the throne proceeded lightnings and thunderings and voices: and there were seven lamps of fire burning before the throne, which are the seven Spirits of God (Rev 4:1-5).

The Church, which holds the vision of the Throne of God in thanksgiving, love, and worship, now enters into Heaven's offering of praise; and, as we acknowledge the authority and the rights of our Creator, we kneel and cast all of our earthly crowns before Him.

And the four beasts had each of them six wings about him; and they were full of eyes within: and they rest not day and night, saying, Holy, holy, holy, Lord God Almighty, which was, and is, and is to come.

And when those beasts give glory and honour and thanks to him that sat on the throne, who liveth for ever and ever,

The four and twenty elders fall down before him that sat on the throne, and worship him that liveth for ever and ever, and cast their crowns before the throne, saying,

Thou art worthy, O Lord, to receive glory and honour and power: for thou hast created all things, and for thy pleasure they are and were created (Rev 4:8-11).

Our attention is directed now to the Lamb that was slain as He opens the understanding of Scripture to us: 1. The History, the Law and the Prophets of the Old Testament; 2. The books of Wisdom and Psalms of the Old Testament; 3. the Letters of the Apostles (and including the Revelation itself); along with the four

Gospels—which when read together, demonstrate that the whole of the Bible is but a single mystery which can only be revealed and understood through the Sacrifice of this Lamb.

Whenever and wherever Scripture is read, we enter into the worship of the Angels and of the Saints because Scripture gives us commonality, community and place among even the hosts of Heaven when we kneel to worship. "Falling down" now, we kneel once more before the only One Who is worthy to open understanding to us. The seven lamps of fire are the Church and the seven Spirits of God are manifested by the Holy Spirit within us—the horns of the Lamb reference power, the eyes wisdom. The commands to "come!" and to "come and see!" are to the whole of the church throughout the whole of the vision:

> And I beheld, and, lo, in the midst of the throne and of the four beasts, and in the midst of the elders, stood a Lamb as it had been slain, having seven horns and seven eyes, which are the seven Spirits of God sent forth into all the earth. (Rev 5:6).

> And every creature which is in heaven, and on the earth, and under the earth, and such as are in the sea, and all that are in them, heard I saying, Blessing, and honour, and glory, and power, be unto him that sitteth upon the throne, and unto the Lamb for ever and ever.

And the four beasts said, Amen. And the four and twenty elders fell down and worshipped him that liveth for ever and ever (Rev 5:13-14).

And I saw when the Lamb opened one of the seals, and I heard, as it were the noise of thunder, one of the four beasts saying, Come and see (Rev 6:1).

By understanding and knowing, the Christ of our Salvation, the Church teaches and guards the truths of the faith in Scripture through preaching, sermon, creed, song and worship. She also proclaims the consequences of rejecting such a great and costly love—and as she experiences the fruits of the mercies of God for herself and offers these mercies to others, she also warns of the judgments of God as she watches those judgments increasingly pour forth from the opening of the seals of Scripture and of Prophecy. We are told to expect persecution for our beliefs, our faithfulness, and our perseverance in witnessing to the truth of God:

And when he had opened the fifth seal, I saw under the altar the souls of them that were slain for the word of God, and for the testimony which they held:

And they cried with a loud voice, saying, How long, O Lord, holy and true, dost thou not judge and avenge our blood on them that dwell on the earth? And white robes were given unto every one of them; and it was said unto them, that they should rest yet for a little season, until their fellow servants also and their brethren, that should be killed as they were, should be fulfilled (Rev 6:9-11).

The Church then observes a holy silence as she offers her life to God and prepares herself to receive the Lamb. This is the Wedding Feast whereby our Covenant and our salvation are consummated. The Church is comforted in her tribulations with this vision of her final salvation and sanctification. We were created to live within the embrace of God and it is only here that we find rest for our souls—and family with one another. How could we not fall down in awe and gratitude for this, the greatest love of all? So now, the Church kneels once more before her Creator as she is sealed with "the seal of the living God."

> After this I beheld, and, lo, a great multitude, which no man could number, of all nations, and kindreds, and people, and tongues, stood before the throne, and before the Lamb, clothed with white robes, and palms in their hands;

> And cried with a loud voice, saying, Salvation to our God which sitteth upon the throne, and unto the Lamb.

> And all the angels stood round about the throne, and about the elders and the four beasts, and fell before the throne on their faces, and worshipped God,

> Saying, Amen: Blessing, and glory, and wisdom, and thanksgiving, and honour, and power, and might, be unto our God for ever and ever. Amen (Rev 7:9-12)

Who kneels beside you when you worship at the Table of the Lord? Can you not see that great cloud of timeless witnesses who stand shoulder to shoulder with you every time you partake of Holy Communion? Can you not hear the angels and the elders singing God's praises as they participate in our worship? Can you not bring yourself to glance through that open doorway and see the immensity of the Heavenly Host there present with you, those who rejoice within the Universal Church when she worships? And every time we sing the song that only the redeemed can know, that song of Thanksgiving for the gift of our Salvation and the gift of God Himself— this is My Body, this is My Blood—we also participate in the Eucharist celebration of offering the whole of ourselves to God in gratitude for it.

And one of the elders answered, saying unto me, What are these which are arrayed in white robes? And whence came they?

And I said unto him, Sir, thou knowest. And he said to me, These are they which came out of great tribulation, and have washed their robes, and made them white in the blood of the Lamb.

Therefore are they before the throne of God, and serve him day and night in his temple: and he that sitteth on the throne shall dwell among them.

They shall hunger no more, neither thirst any more; neither shall the sun light on them, nor any heat.

For the Lamb which is in the midst of the throne shall feed them, and shall lead them unto living fountains of waters: and God shall wipe away all tears from their eyes (Rev 7:13-17).

The Church intercedes for others as the prayers of the Church become the incense of Heaven.

And when he had opened the seventh seal, there was silence in heaven about the space of half an hour.

And I saw the seven angels which stood before God; and to them were given seven trumpets.

And another angel came and stood at the altar, having a golden censer; and there was given unto him much incense, that he should offer it with the prayers of all saints upon the golden altar which was before the throne.

And the smoke of the incense, which came with the prayers of the saints, ascended up before God out of the angel's hand (Rev 8:1-4).

Now, as we recite the Lord's Prayer, we forgive and ask forgiveness of our brothers and sisters as we are reconciled, and the Bride has made Herself ready to receive the Bridegroom:

We have acknowledged the real presence of Christ within our worship.

We have repented of and confessed our sins.

We have listened to and understood the fullness of the blessings and warnings of Scripture as it is opened up to us by the Lamb that was slain.

We have interceded for others.

We have forgiven those who have harmed us and others and asked for forgiveness in return.

We now acknowledge in thanksgiving, the presence of Christ in the bread and the wine of the Eucharistic celebration. It is finally time for the Marriage Feast of the Lamb.

PART II: HOLY COMMUNION

The Church prepares and the Holy Spirit consecrates the Bread and the Wine of the Holy Communion as the Altar of Heaven descends upon and sanctifies the altar of the Church on earth. And as the Bridegroom gives of Himself to the Bride, the Bride offers herself to the Bridegroom, at the Altar of Sacrifice, the consummation of the Wedding Feast of the Lamb.

> And I heard as it were the voice of a great multitude, and as the voice of many waters, and as the voice of mighty thunderings, saying, Alleluia: for the Lord God omnipotent reigneth.
>
> Let us be glad and rejoice, and give honour to him: for the marriage of the Lamb is come, and his wife hath made herself ready.

And to her was granted that she should be arrayed in fine linen, clean and white: for the fine linen is the righteousness of saints.

And he saith unto me, Write, Blessed are they which are called unto the marriage supper of the Lamb. And he saith unto me, These are the true sayings of God.

And I fell at his feet to worship him. And he said unto me, See thou do it not: I am thy fellowservant, and of thy brethren that have the testimony of Jesus: worship God: for the testimony of Jesus is the spirit of prophecy (Rev 19:6-10).

And as they were eating, Jesus took bread, and blessed it, and brake it, and gave it to the disciples, and said, Take, eat; this is my body.

And he took the cup, and gave thanks, and gave it to them, saying, Drink ye all of it;

For this is my blood of the new testament, which is shed for many for the remission of sins (Matt 26: 26-28).

Is the Marriage Supper of the Lamb just a remembrance? Or is our Holy Communion a miraculous multiplication of the Last Supper? Take and eat, this is my body. Take and drink, this is my blood.

But he said unto them, Give ye them to eat. And they said, We have no more but five loaves and two fishes; except we should go and buy meat for all this people.

For they were about five thousand men. And he said to his disciples, Make them sit down by fifties in a company.

And they did so, and made them all sit down.

Then he took the five loaves and the two fishes, and looking up to heaven, he blessed them, and brake, and gave to the disciples to set before the multitude.

And they did eat, and were all filled: and there was taken up of fragments that remained to them twelve baskets (Luke 9:13-17).

What was. What is. What is to come. The always present of the now of Heaven becomes our always present here on earth.

And I John saw the holy city, new Jerusalem, coming down from God out of heaven, prepared as a bride adorned for her husband (Rev 21:2).

And there came unto me one of the seven angels which had the seven vials full of the seven last plagues, and talked with me, saying, Come hither, I will shew thee the bride, the Lamb's wife.

And he carried me away in the spirit to a great and high mountain, and shewed me that great city, the holy

Jerusalem, descending out of heaven from God (Rev 21:9-10).

And I saw no temple therein: for the Lord God Almighty and the Lamb are the temple of it.

And the city had no need of the sun, neither of the moon, to shine in it: for the glory of God did lighten it, and the Lamb is the light thereof.

And the nations of them which are saved shall walk in the light of it: and the kings of the earth do bring their glory and honour into it.

And the gates of it shall not be shut at all by day: for there shall be no night there.

And they shall bring the glory and honour of the nations into it.

And there shall in no wise enter into it any thing that defileth, neither whatsoever worketh abomination, or maketh a lie: but they which are written in the Lamb's book of life (Rev 21:22-27).

The Church does not change or alter either Scripture or the understanding of Scripture, in any way, not by word and not by interpretation and not by fictionalized renderings of Scripture—and that includes the whole of Scripture. We read and understand the whole of the Bible by accepting and reading the whole of the Bible, period. That which has been revealed to us by the Lamb of

God Himself is sacred Scripture and we are standing on hallowed ground when we read it, when we hear it, when we celebrate it; and when we receive it. This is the Word of the Lord. Thanks be to God.

> Behold, I come quickly: blessed is he that keepeth the sayings of the prophecy of this book (Rev 22:7).

Heaven descends in Christ and earth ascends to meet Him at the consecration of the bread and the wine when God, in fact, and in truth, folds space as He offers Himself to us again and again in the multiplication of Holy Communion—just as He multiplied the wine and the fishes on the mountain. This is the Marriage Feast of the Lamb. This is the true rapture. This is the vision of the liturgy that John saw on the Lord's Day. Thanks be to God.

Christ now sends us forth with a blessing so that the world might be blessed through us as we work and wait for His always imminent return.

18

GOD'S ABSOLUTE AUTHORITY

THE TWO CITIES

1. Within John's Revelation, God confirms and demonstrates His total, unquestionable and absolute authority. This is the New Jerusalem.

2. With this vision, we can see ourselves as a unique and personal creation whose destiny can only be fulfilled in the eternal Communion of Heaven. This is the New Jerusalem.

3. Gifted with Revelation, we can see the worship of Heaven so that we can establish that same pattern for our adoration here on earth. We share together and are at-one-with all of the faithful servants of God in the joy and in the delight of the presence of God—that same Triune God Who not only lives among us but lives within us, even here on earth. This also is the New Jerusalem.

4. Now, the Revelation brings us back to the beginning, back to the first chapters of this book and back to the Book of Genesis, even back to before the beginning of the Creation itself.

The third dynamic mystery takes up the understanding of a reality in which humanity must choose between two cities: The New Jerusalem (The City of God); and Babylon (The City of Man). These two cities are the two antitypes of their types in the Creation stories of Genesis: Adam (male and female), created from the Breath of God, and mankind (male and female), which became so wicked that they had to be utterly destroyed. It is still all about the authority of God over what He has created and our freedom to choose whether we will go on to a greater existence in Him or retreat into the primordial darkness of chaos once more.

> But this thing commanded I them, saying, Obey my voice, and I will be your God, and ye shall be my people: and walk ye in all the ways that I have commanded you, that it may be well unto you.

> But they hearkened not, nor inclined their ear, but walked in the counsels and in the imagination of their evil heart, and went backward, and not forward (Jer 7: 23-24).

The first Biblical hint of the existence of the two cities in exact opposition to each other is when God separates the light from the darkness and calls the light "good."

> In the beginning God created the heaven and the earth.

> And the earth was without form, and void; and darkness was upon the face of the deep. And the Spirit of God moved upon the face of the waters.

And God said, Let there be light: and there was light.

And God saw the light, that it was good: and God divided the light from the darkness.

And God called the light Day, and the darkness he called Night. And the evening and the morning were the first day (Gen 1:1-5).

The second indication was His promise to the Serpent after the original fall of Adam and Eve, the promise of a Messiah, the Savior of Mankind.

And I will put enmity between thee and the woman, and between thy seed and her seed; it shall bruise thy head, and thou shalt bruise his heel (Gen 3:15).

The third demonstration of light and darkness, good and evil, the struggle of obedience with disobedience is in that which God revealed to Cain:

If thou doest well, shalt thou not be accepted? and if thou doest not well, sin lieth at the door (Gen 4:7).

Cain responds to God by killing his brother.

And he said, What hast thou done? the voice of thy brother's blood crieth unto me from the ground.

And now art thou cursed from the earth, which hath opened her mouth to receive thy brother's blood from thy hand (Gen 4:10-11).

Then the flood came when things simply went from bad to worse. So bad, in fact, that there was nothing left to do but to start mankind all over again. Dry land appears, everyone gets off the ark, the memory of the flood fades and the same old problem begins all over again. One of Noah's sons, Ham, sins against his father and is cursed for it. Two generations later, a grandson of Ham by the name of Nimrod becomes a great and mighty evil throughout the land—and it was this type of his antitype, Lucifer, of whom Babel was born and the City of Babylon which sprouted from her foul roots.

> And Cush begat Nimrod: he began to be a mighty one in the earth.
>
> He was a mighty hunter before the Lord: wherefore it is said, Even as Nimrod the mighty hunter before the Lord.
>
> And the beginning of his kingdom was Babel, and Erech, and Accad, and Calneh, in the land of Shinar.
>
> Out of that land went forth Asshur, and builded Nineveh, and the city Rehoboth, and Calah,
>
> And Resen between Nineveh and Calah: the same is a great city (Gen 10:8-12).

Nimrod challenged God, turned his power into tyranny and wanted not only to be his own god but everyone else's god.

How art thou fallen from heaven, O Lucifer, son of the morning! how art thou cut down to the ground, which didst weaken the nations!

For thou hast said in thine heart,

I will ascend into heaven,

I will exalt my throne above the stars of God:

I will sit also upon the mount of the congregation, in the sides of the north:

I will ascend above the heights of the clouds;

I will be like the most High (Isa 14:12-14).

Lucifer says "I will" five times in the above passages, therefore despising the authority of his Maker and setting himself up as his own authority—this was the first sin and the ancestor of every sin after it: "my will be done!"

Babylon is that city of the Sixth Day which sits atop the seven mountains and oceans of the earth: Asia, Africa, North America, South America, Antarctica, Europe, and Australia, i.e., the number seven once again, which encompasses the whole of the earth. There is no place on earth where Lucifer's Babylon, the "great whore that sitteth upon many waters," cannot be found and thinking that it only rules over Europe or that it only rules from one city in this world is without reason—the rebellious rule of Lucifer is evident wherever life is found.

And there came one of the seven angels which had the seven vials, and talked with me, saying unto me, Come hither; I will shew unto thee the judgment of the great whore that sitteth upon many waters:

With whom the kings of the earth have committed fornication, and the inhabitants of the earth have been made drunk with the wine of her fornication.

So he carried me away in the spirit into the wilderness: and I saw a woman sit upon a scarlet coloured beast, full of names of blasphemy, having seven heads and ten horns.

And the woman was arrayed in purple and scarlet colour, and decked with gold and precious stones and pearls, having a golden cup in her hand full of abominations and filthiness of her fornication:

And upon her forehead was a name written, Mystery, Babylon The Great, The Mother Of Harlots And Abominations Of The Earth.

And I saw the woman drunken with the blood of the saints, and with the blood of the martyrs of Jesus: and when I saw her, I wondered with great admiration (Rev 17:1-6).

In John's revelation, we see that Babylon is a sort of Frankenstein city made up of the spiritually dead. It was born in order to hold those who would fall into Lucifer's own rebellion. It is a patchwork kingdom that is already doomed, complete with its own fallen angels and all of those who have chosen their own authority over the authority of God. To those of us who are still having to live with the horror of this kingdom in time, it is a bit overpowering, so we need to finish those verses that we started in Isaiah 14 and look at it from God's perspective again, from the Throne of His Judgment:

> Yet thou shalt be brought down to hell, to the sides of the pit.

> They that see thee shall narrowly look upon thee, and consider thee, saying, Is this the man that made the earth to tremble, that did shake kingdoms;

> That made the world as a wilderness, and destroyed the cities thereof; that opened not the house of his prisoners?

> All the kings of the nations, even all of them, lie in glory, every one in his own house.

> But thou art cast out of thy grave like an abominable branch, and as the raiment of those that are slain, thrust through with a sword, that go down to the stones of the pit; as a carcase trodden under feet.

> Thou shalt not be joined with them in burial, because thou hast destroyed thy land, and slain thy people: the seed of evildoers shall never be renowned (Isa 14:15-20).

God's judgment upon Babylon is fatal and final as He destroys His enemies and ours once and for all:

Come, behold the works of the Lord, what desolations he hath made in the earth.

He maketh wars to cease unto the end of the earth; he breaketh the bow, and cutteth the spear in sunder; he burneth the chariot in the fire.

Be still, and know that I am God: I will be exalted among the heathen, I will be exalted in the earth.

The Lord of hosts is with us; the God of Jacob is our refuge. Selah (Ps 46:8-11)

There is a final end to the city of Babylon, the city which refuses the authority of God. We are told to "Be still, and know that I am God" and to wait patiently for it.

And he cried mightily with a strong voice, saying, Babylon the great is fallen, is fallen, and is become the habitation of devils, and the hold of every foul spirit, and a cage of every unclean and hateful bird (Rev 18:2).

We are warned again and again not to take part in her sins or to do business with her:

And I heard another voice from heaven, saying, Come out of her, my people, that ye be not partakers of her sins, and that ye receive not of her plagues.

For her sins have reached unto heaven, and God hath remembered her iniquities (Rev 18:4-5).

Where Christ is, the whole of His Church is there present with Him as time is taken up into Eternity and becomes, inseparably and forever, joined together. The New Jerusalem is the Bride of Christ made pure, perfect, holy and beautiful by His sacrificial love for us. She is the faithful city. She is the faithful spouse.

It is in the folding of space and within the transparency and in the permeability of the Creation that the Church of Heaven kneels to lift up the Church on earth as they worship their Lord in the New Jerusalem, the City of God.

And when the servant of the man of God was risen early, and gone forth, behold, an host compassed the city both with horses and chariots. And his servant said unto him, Alas, my master! how shall we do?

And he answered, Fear not: for they that be with us are more than they that be with them.

And Elisha prayed, and said, Lord, I pray thee, open his eyes, that he may see. And the Lord opened the eyes of the young man; and he saw: and, behold, the mountain was full of horses and chariots of fire round about Elisha (2 Kings 6:15-17).

And he shewed me a pure river of water of life, clear as crystal, proceeding out of the throne of God and of the Lamb.

In the midst of the street of it, and on either side of the river, was there the tree of life, which bare twelve manner of fruits, and yielded her fruit every month: and the leaves of the tree were for the healing of the nations.

And there shall be no more curse: but the throne of God and of the Lamb shall be in it; and his servants shall serve him:

And they shall see his face; and his name shall be in their foreheads.

And there shall be no night there; and they need no candle, neither light of the sun; for the Lord God giveth them light: and they shall reign for ever and ever (Rev 22:1-5).

SECTION VII

BEING CHRISTIAN IN A SIXTH

DAY WORLD

And let the beauty of the Lord our God be upon us: and establish thou the work of our hands upon us; yea, the work of our hands establish thou it (Ps 90:17).

WOUNDS

BE NOT AFRAID

I came across a most insightful article regarding the wounds of the risen Christ. The commentary that so touched me was "Glorious Wounds—Christ's and Ours," written by Fr. Andrew Hofer, O.P.[1] Central to the article was the question of why the Risen Christ was not healed of His wounds—for what reason did His glorified body still present the marks of His crucifixion? To which Fr. Hofer gives five Aquinas answers (by way of the Venerable Bede), which are here represented but greatly modified, and perhaps, over-simplified, from the original documents.

Jesus displays his mortal wounds:

1. for the glory of Christ Himself in demonstration of His obedience to the Father;

2. for concrete evidence of his death and subsequent resurrection;

3. for interposition between the Father and the sinner as Christ's intercession for us;

4. as a sign of God's Divine Mercy to sinners;

5. and as a sign of God's Judgment upon those who have refused God's Divine Mercy.

> Behold my hands and my feet, that it is I myself: handle me, and see; for a spirit hath not flesh and bones, as ye see me have (Luke 24:39).

"Let me see your resurrection wounds," we can demand of all the want-to-be messiahs. Those five mortal wounds, which cannot be duplicated because they died with, were buried with and were resurrected with Christ's glorified body so that we might be healed and made whole by the marks and the stripes of His sacrificial wounds.

> Then saith he to Thomas, Reach hither thy finger, and behold my hands; and reach hither thy hand, and thrust it into my side: and be not faithless, but believing (John 20:27).

"Let me see your wounds," the resurrected Christ says to us today. We should also be carrying the marks of our Lord upon ourselves. If we are on a battlefield and in the middle of a fierce battle, we will be wounded. We are left here in this Sixth Day in order to carry on Christ's work on behalf of the soul of Adam. God expects us to love, to suffer, to be rejected, and even to be killed—

murdered because we are not only the sign of God's love and mercy to the world, but we champion His ownership and authority over all of His Creation. Physically, emotionally, spiritually, and even mentally, we will be wounded, we will be torn, and our hearts will be broken. We will have wounds to show Him, now, and at His coming again.

> And when he had called the people unto him with his disciples also, he said unto them, Whosoever will come after me, let him deny himself, and take up his cross, and follow me.

> For whosoever will save his life shall lose it; but whosoever shall lose his life for my sake and the gospel's, the same shall save it (Mark 8:34-35).

"If you love, you will suffer," the Priest repeated five times from the pulpit for emphasis that morning. "If you love, you will suffer." That was the only message that he gave us, but no explanation for it was asked or needed. "If you love, you will suffer." To follow Christ is to love. "If you love, you will suffer." To love is to offer ourselves in sacrifice as Christ offered Himself. To love is to be wounded, is to suffer. But never are we left alone when we join our sufferings to the sufferings of Christ for this world that He loves so very much. "If you love, you will suffer."

> Jesus answered and said unto him, If a man love me, he will keep my words: and my Father will love him, and we will come unto him, and make our abode with him.

He that loveth me not keepeth not my sayings: and the word which ye hear is not mine, but the Father's which sent me.

These things have I spoken unto you, being yet present with you.

But the Comforter, which is the Holy Ghost, whom the Father will send in my name, he shall teach you all things, and bring all things to your remembrance, whatsoever I have said unto you.

Peace I leave with you, my peace I give unto you: not as the world giveth, give I unto you. Let not your heart be troubled, neither let it be afraid (John 14:23-27).

The answer to fear is not to tell your congregations that there is nothing to fear because there is and they already know it. The answer to fear is personal consecration to and trust in Divine Providence. God is never, ever, not in charge of all that is. God's authority over all of His Creation is the only true authority that exists. Blessed is that Church, which teaches its people that there is meaning in their sufferings and that they will have to suffer in this fallen world. Blessed is the Church that teaches its people to obstinately persevere both in times of sorrow and in times of joy, for they are both only tools in the hand of God. And blessed is the Church that consecrates its people to the will of their Lord.

The first subtitle chosen for this book was: *Christians Living in a Sixth Day World:* but it wasn't long before I realized that we could load our little cart with all the faith, hope and love that it can carry, but it takes the workhorse team of blind trust and obstinate obedience to pull that precious cargo through the deserts of time and us to the other side of it. _Being Christian in a Sixth Day World_ goes deeper than 'what' we are—it gets down to 'who' we are now and 'who' we are becoming, the sons and the daughters of a living God and the Bride of His Christ. Trust and obedience are the heart that pumps life into our faith, hope and love, even when we don't understand what is happening—_especially when we don't understand._

> Trust in the Lord with all thine heart; and lean not unto thine own understanding. In all thy ways acknowledge him, and he shall direct thy paths (Prov 3:5-6).

What keeps you from consecrating your life, your will and all that belongs to you, to God? Fear? Lack of trust? Worried about what God will ask of you and if you will have the strength to do it? You are justified, but are you sanctified? You lead a good Christian life, but have you let the Christ of God die on the cross of your justification and not be resurrected again within you, which is your sanctification? Have you taken the time to meet your living Savior in the here and now? To feel His Presence? To listen to His Voice? Do you welcome His touch when the finger of God presses hard and painfully upon you? Are you worried that your own dreams will have to be given up and nailed to Calvary's Cross?

And are you so concerned about wounds that you cannot come into the fullness of the life that God has planned for you?

Christ calls our wounds blessed in the Beatitudes, but we must complete their blessing by freely offering them up again and again to God to use for His purposes. Our wounds are powerful intercessors. They are like a mighty army when they are in the hands of God—so do not waste a single one of them.

What would Jesus do? Jesus, as you well know, would pray.

STANDING IN THE GAP

WHILE WE WAIT FOR HIS RETURN

And the men turned their faces from thence, and went toward Sodom: but Abraham stood yet before the Lord.

And Abraham drew near, and said, Wilt thou also destroy the righteous with the wicked?

Peradventure there be fifty righteous within the city: wilt thou also destroy and not spare the place for the fifty righteous that are therein?

That be far from thee to do after this manner, to slay the righteous with the wicked: and that the righteous should be as the wicked, that be far from thee: Shall not the Judge of all the earth do right?

And the Lord said, If I find in Sodom fifty righteous within the city, then I will spare all the place for their sakes (Gen 18:22-26).

If we follow this most famous of intercessions to the end, Abraham intercedes for the city down to ten righteous souls, which were agreed to by God; but even at ten, the city could not be saved. Only Lot and his family were brought out of the city before it was destroyed.

Christ intercedes. The Holy Spirit intercedes. The Saints intercede. The Christian, therefore, intercedes.

Are we willing to do what Christians have always done before us, something they used to call "standing in the gap?" Are we willing to do what it takes to intercede for those who are lost by standing with Jesus between the sinner and the justice of God, begging for the mercy of God? Are we willing to do what it takes to "stand in the gap" for family, for friends, for nation—for the whole of the world of Adam? Jesus asks that His followers take up their crosses and follow Him *now*. No Bibles hidden to be found later—because there is no later. No recordings stuffed under mattresses or left on closet shelves. The Millennium Reign of Christ is now, but the Great Tribulation is also now, and it is increasing. Wherever Christ is, there must be His Bride also, and as Christ is standing in the gap for us, so must we also stand in the gap for others. While we wait for His return, prayer is the foremost work of the Church.

But today's Christians are like the disciples were before the Pentecostal fire of the Holy Spirit fell upon them, for it is always when the fields are ripest for the harvest that we want to run away and hide. Perhaps we need to return to that upper room again and pray until the Holy Spirit pours Himself out upon all of Christendom with a new Pentecostal fire. Pray that we will be filled and empowered as soldiers of Christ so that we might witness to, and fight for, Adam's dying world. Yet, it is not the Holy Spirit Who must be awakened with our prayers; it is Christ's sleepy Bride that must be shaken, and if it takes our discomfort to rouse us, then discomfort will come.

"Come Holy Spirit and renew the face of the earth!"

We are His martyrs. We are His witnesses to the world of God's design for the Creation. We will not forsake Him in His hour of greatest need. And when the entire world deserts us and the darkness descends, and we feel that we are alone—He is right here within us, and surrounding us, holding and upholding us.

God is our Father, our 'Abba', our Spouse, our Friend, Comforter, Guide, our Light, and the very Love and Longing of our being. We have been chosen. We are family in Him and family with one another—and when we gather together in worship of Him, we *all* become one in Him. What a great treasure we are given through our Lord, the Image of God within us as we pray to be filled with the fullness of His Presence—and how tragic it is when we reject Him! It's as simple as that. All is ready, and everything is provided for us, but He cannot give that which will not be received. This cannot be repeated enough—the unforgiveable sin against the Holy Spirit is simply to refuse Him.

Call unto me, and I will answer thee, and show thee great and mighty things, which thou knowest not (Jer 33:3).

Too many of today's Christians want to call down the wrath of God upon the earth—but it is not Pentecostal Fire that they desire, it is judgmental fire and these Christians are yearning for Armageddon. They aren't looking for the salvation of the world; they are just looking for a way to escape its troubles.

And it came to pass, when the time was come that he should be received up, he stedfastly set his face to go to Jerusalem,

And sent messengers before his face: and they went, and entered into a village of the Samaritans, to make ready for him.

And they did not receive him, because his face was as though he would go to Jerusalem.

And when his disciples James and John saw this, they said, Lord, wilt thou that we command fire to come down from heaven, and consume them, even as Elias did?

But he turned, and rebuked them, and said, Ye know not what manner of spirit ye are of.

For the Son of man is not come to destroy men's lives, but to save them. And they went to another village (Luke 9: 51-56).

All of Judeo-Christianity is commanded to pray for the soul of mankind, feed the poor, minister to the sick and save what we can of the race of Adam. In God's house of many rooms and long corridors, can we not find at least one meeting room in which we can gather? Even for a day, can we not pray together for our deeply troubled nation? For the world?

> And John answered and said, Master, we saw one casting out devils in thy name; and we forbad him, because he followeth not with us.
>
> And Jesus said unto him, Forbid him not: for he that is not against us is for us (Luke 9:49-50).

Here are five clues to the mystery of the parable of the Ten Virgins:

1. Ten is the ecclesiastical number of the whole.

2. Five is the ecclesiastical number of God's grace, and the oil that the wise carry within their lamps is the chrism oil of the Holy Spirit by which they are anointed—and this same oil which seals their covenant with God brings them also into the fullness of Grace, which is the fire of the Holy Spirit blazing within them. The five foolish virgins have let that fire burn out within them.

Thomas Aquinas gives us the five effects of grace upon us: *first*, that the soul is healed; *second*, that it wills what is good; *third*, that it carries out what it wills; *fourth*, that it perseveres in good; and *fifth*, that it attains to glory.[1]

3. There are five wounds of Christ's obedience that accomplished our salvation.

4. A falling asleep almost always refers to death in Scripture, but it seems to have a three-fold message here: *first*, those in whom the life of the Holy Spirit has gone out in the long awaiting for His return; *second*, those in whom the oil of the Holy Spirit within them is kindled into a flaming fire at the nearness of His coming, and; *third*, those who have physically died but are raised to life again at Christ's coming. (Remember, there is no time in Eternity.)

5. When Christ comes to bring His Bride to her new home, He comes but once, and then the door is shut, closed forever.

> Then shall the kingdom of heaven be likened unto ten virgins, which took their lamps, and went forth to meet the bridegroom.
>
> And five of them were wise, and five were foolish.
>
> They that were foolish took their lamps, and took no oil with them:
>
> But the wise took oil in their vessels with their lamps.
>
> While the bridegroom tarried, they all slumbered and slept (Matt 25:1-5).

You know how this story ends. Those who had kept the faith and prepared for His return went in with the Bridegroom to the Marriage Feast. Those who did not were locked out forever. This parable is surrounded and reinforced by numerous parables and prophecies of the last days (days which promise persecution for the Bride of Christ and for the whole of Judeo-Christianity on earth). Every parable of the last days encourages us to prepare for these days. Once again, there is no later with God—there is only the eternal now.

> Who then is a faithful and wise servant, whom his lord hath made ruler over his household, to give them meat in due season?
>
> Blessed is that servant, whom his lord when he cometh shall find so doing.
>
> Verily I say unto you, That he shall make him ruler over all his goods.
>
> But and if that evil servant shall say in his heart, My lord delayeth his coming;
>
> And shall begin to smite his fellowservants, and to eat and drink with the drunken;
>
> The lord of that servant shall come in a day when he looketh not for him, and in an hour that he is not aware of, And shall cut him asunder, and appoint him his portion with the hypocrites: there shall be weeping and gnashing of teeth (Matt 24:45-51).

The parable of the 10 virgins fulfills the final definition of the Marriage Feast of the Lamb when the life that was given to us in the beginning of our faith is taken up into the very Life of God Himself.

> And while they went to buy, the bridegroom came; and they that were ready went in with him to the marriage: and the door was shut.
>
> Afterward came also the other virgins, saying, Lord, Lord, open to us.
>
> But he answered and said, Verily I say unto you, I know you not.
>
> Watch therefore, for ye know neither the day nor the hour wherein the Son of man cometh (Matt 25:10-13).

Come Holy Spirit and renew the face of the Earth!

> The Spirit and the bride say, Come. And let him that heareth say, Come. And let him that is athirst come. And whosoever will, let him take the water of life freely (Rev 22:17).
>
> The grace of our Lord Jesus Christ be with you all. Amen (Rev 22:21).

AUTHOR'S NOTE ON PSALM 90:
THE INTERCESSION OF MOSES

Psalm 90 was divided into seven quotes, each part of which was printed on one of the Seven Section pages of this book. I thought it not only relevant to the book's purposes, but to the times within which we now live.

Lord, thou hast been our dwelling place in all generations.

Before the mountains were brought forth, or ever thou hadst formed the earth and the world, even from everlasting to everlasting, thou art God.

Thou turnest man to destruction; and sayest, Return, ye children of men.

For a thousand years in thy sight are but as yesterday when it is past, and as a watch in the night.

Thou carriest them away as with a flood; they are as a sleep: in the morning they are like grass which groweth up.

In the morning it flourisheth, and groweth up; in the evening it is cut down, and withereth.

For we are consumed by thine anger, and by thy wrath are we troubled.

Thou hast set our iniquities before thee, our secret sins in the light of thy countenance.

For all our days are passed away in thy wrath: we spend our years as a tale that is told.

The days of our years are threescore years and ten; and if by reason of strength they be fourscore years, yet is their strength labour and sorrow; for it is soon cut off, and we fly away.

Who knoweth the power of thine anger? even according to thy fear, so is thy wrath.

So teach us to number our days, that we may apply our hearts unto wisdom.

Return, O Lord, how long? and let it repent thee concerning thy servants.

O satisfy us early with thy mercy; that we may rejoice and be glad all our days.

Make us glad according to the days wherein thou hast afflicted us, and the years wherein we have seen evil.

Let thy work appear unto thy servants, and thy glory unto their children.

And let the beauty of the Lord our God be upon us: and establish thou the work of our hands upon us; yea, the work of our hands establish thou it (Ps 90).

ENDNOTES

THE EIGHTH DAY:

Being Christian In A Sixth Day World

Scripture quotes as noted in text.

INTRODUCTION: THE COMMON BODY OF CHRIST

[1]Herbert Thurston, "Devotion to the Passion of Christ." The Catholic Encyclopedia, Vol.11 (New York: Robert Appleton Company,1911) http://www.newadvent.org/cathen/11527b.htm (14 December 2015).

SECTION I: BEGINNINGS

1. GENESIS, CREATION AND QUINTESSENCE: The Fifth Element

Scripture quotes as noted in text.

2. ARE WE EVOLVING? When God's Authority is Questioned

Scripture quotes as noted in text.

3. THE FLOOD: Type and Antitype in the Bible

[1]Rabbi Jonathan Sacks, *To Heal a Fractured World, The Ethics of Responsibility* (New York: Schocken Books, a Division of Random House, 2005) 134.

[2]John D. Davis, A Dictionary of the Bible, "Chronology" (New Jersey: Fleming H. Revell Company, 1965), 134.

4. MELCHIZEDEK: From the Old Adam to the New Adam

Scripture quotes as noted in text.

SECTION II: COVENANTS

5. HEALING THE WORLD: The Christian Covenant

Scripture quotes as noted in text.

6. THE CHURCH DIVIDED: Burying Hatred

[1]Mohandas K. Gandhi, AUTOBIOGRAPHY: The Story of My Experiments with Truth, unabridged republication (New York: Dover Publications, Inc., 1983) 208. Originally published by Public Affairs Press, Washington, D. C.1948, under the title Gandhi's Autobiography: The Story of My Experiments with Truth.

[2]Timothy Ware, The Orthodox Church, (England: Penguin Books, the Penguin Group, 1997) 324.

[3]Joseph Cardinal Ratzinger, Imprimi Potest, Catechism of the Catholic Church, with Modifications from the Editio Typica, 2nd ed., (New York, London, Toronto, Sydney, Auckland:Doubleday, 1997) #818, 235.

[4]Ibid. #814, 233.

7. LAW AND GRACE: Thesis, Antithesis, and Synthesis; Type, Antitype, and Supersessionism

Scripture quotes as noted in text.

SECTION III: MANIFESTING THE TRINITY

8. THE SIMPLICITY OF GOD: Transcendent, (In)Comprehensible, (Un)Knowable, (In)Visible

[1]Peter Kreeft, A Shorter Summa, The Essential Philosophical Passages of St. Thomas Aquinas Summa Theologica Edited and Explained by Peter Kreeft (San Francisco: Ignatius Press 1993) footnote, 85.

[2]Rev. John Trigilio, Jr. and Rev. Kenneth Brighenti, The Catholicism Answer Book (Sourcebooks, Inc., Naperville, Illinois 2007) 9

9. THE HOLINESS OF GOD: Prayer

[1]Thomas Merton, Life and Holiness (New York, London, Toronto, Sydney, Auckland: Image Books-Doubleday, 1963, 1996) 12.

[2]Ibid. 15.

[3]Ibid.15 (quote from St. John Chrysostom's Homily xvi on Ephesians).

[4]Brother Lawrence (Nicholas Herman) The Practice of the Presence of God with Spiritual Maxims (Grand Rapids, Michigan: Fleming H. Revell, Published by Spire Books a Division of Baker Publishing Group, 2006) 36-37.

[5]C. S. Lewis, Mere Christianity (Harper San Francisco, Division of Harper Collins Publishers, 2001) 198-199.

10. COME, HOLY SPIRIT: Renewing the Face of the Earth

Scripture quotes as noted in text.

SECTION IV: THE END IS THE BEGINNING

11. THE NUMBERING OF OUR DAYS: Jude's Prelude to John's Song

Scripture quotes as noted in text.

SECTION V: JOHN'S REVELATION

12. INTRODUCTION TO REVELATION: Things to Remember

[1]St. Augustine, The City of God (Book XI) Chapter 25, Of the Division of Philosophy into Three Parts, translated by Marcus Dods. From Nicene and Post-Nicene Fathers, First Series,

Vol. 2. Edited by Philip Schaff. (Buffalo, NY: Christian Literature Publishing Co., 1887.) Revised and edited for New Advent by Kevin Knight http://www.newadvent.org/fathers/120111.htm, (15 December 2015).

13. THE STRUCTURE OF THE CREATION: Divisions and Meanings

[1]John D. Davis, A Dictionary of the Bible, "Revelation" (New Jersey: Fleming H. Revell Company, 1965), 652-654.

14. THE NUMBERS OF HEAVEN: The Dominion of Christ

Scripture quotes as noted in text.

15. THE NUMBERS OF MANKIND: The Seven Days of the Creation

[1]St. Ambrose 340-397 Bishop of Milan and Doctor of the Church (On the Holy Spirit, Book I, Chapter XVI) 177 -179 Christian Classics Ethereal Library

NPNF2-10. Ambrose: Selected Works and Letters

http://www.ccel.org/ccel/schaff/npnf210.iv.ii.ii.xvii.html?hi ghlight=ambrose,river,spirit#highlight , (15 December 2015).

SECTION VI: THE EIGHTH DAY

16. THE BRIDE OF THE NEW CREATION: The Eighth Day

Scripture quotes as noted in text.

17. THE LITURGY OF HEAVEN AND EARTH: The New Jerusalem

Scripture quotes as noted in text.

18. GOD'S ABSOLUTE AUTHORITY: The Two Cities

Scripture quotes as noted in text.

SECTION VII: BEING CHRISTIAN IN A SIXTH DAY WORLD

19. WOUNDS: Be Not Afraid

[1]Andrew Hofer, O.P., "Glorious Wounds—Christ's and Ours," Homiletic & Pastoral Review, Ignatius Press, (posted April 9, 2013), http://www.hprweb.com/2013/04/glorious-wounds-christs-and-ours, (accessed 24 April 2013).

20. STANDING IN THE GAP: While We Wait for His Return

[1]Thomas Aquinas, Nature and Grace: Selections from the Summa Theologica of Thomas Aquinas, Art. Three of Question 111: pg 169, Whether Grace is Appropriately Divided into Prevenient and Subsequent Grace. Christian Classics Ethereal Library http://www.ccel.org/ccel/aquinas/nature_grace.viii.iii.iii.html, (15 December 2015).